Biblical Counseling:
Essential to the Development of a Truck Stop Ministry

A Doctoral Project
Submitted to the D. Min. Studies Committee of
Charlotte Theological Seminary
Charlotte, North Carolina

In Partial Fulfillment
of the Requirements for the Degree Doctor of
Ministry

Julie Anne Smith

Parson's Porch Books

Biblical Counseling: Essential to the Development of a Truck Stop Ministry
ISBN: Softcover 978-1-960326-96-6
Copyright © 2024 by Julie Anne Smith

Cover Credit: Thanks to Cassandra Rene' Phillips for her contribution to the cover.

Photo Credit: Photos of Julie Anne Smith by Vjara Lezah

Parson's Porch Books is an imprint of Parson's Porch *&* Company (PP*&*C) in Cleveland, Tennessee. PP*&*C is a self-funded charity which earns money by publishing books of noted authors, representing all genres. Its face and voice is **David Russell Tullock** (dtullock@parsonsporch.com).

Parson's Porch *&* Company *turns books into bread & milk* by sharing its profits with the poor.

www.parsonsporch.com

Biblical Counseling:
Essential to the Development of a Truck Stop Ministry

Contents

Chapter One...6

   Introduction

Chapter Two 23

   Literature Review

Chapter Three 31

   Research Methodologies

Chapter Four..74

   Evangelism

Chapter Five.. 102

   Understanding the Central Organ of the Body: The Brain

Chapter Six 108

   Drug Addictions

Chapter Seven 117

   Brain Addictions

Chapter Eight.. 120

   Body Addictions

Chapter Nine... 124

   Trucking Industry

Chapter Ten... 134

   Conclusion

Appendix One.. 140

   Informed Consent

Bibliography 142

Chapter One

Introduction

The purpose of this dissertation is to provide an overview of the doctoral research project. This doctoral project is an extension of the master's thesis written as a fulfillment of the Master of Divinity Degree Program. The original project focused on developing a practical Truck Stop Ministry. However, evangelism is one of the essential aspects of discipleship. Therefore, to provide a more detailed training tool for the ministry, the current project will discuss the importance of biblical counseling and addictions, which have increased over the past year in the trucking community. According to Prepress, data from the Federal Motor Carrier Safety Administration's Drug and Alcohol Clearinghouse shows a 10.2% increase in 58,215 drug violations in 2021.[1]

The introduction focuses on increasing the reader's insight while providing an overview of the book. This chapter aims to break down the different processes and research methods used to prepare the book, beginning with an introduction and ending with a conclusion demonstrating the importance of the doctoral project. Luke 14:23 is the focal Scripture for this dissertation. As it pertains to society today, this ministry requires a person to go out into the highways to speak to a community; secluded and forgotten in society.

Twelve years ago, I married my husband, who had worked in the trucking industry for 37 years. I did not understand or have an actual community perspective at the time. As time passed, I noticed something missing at the truck stops. Many truck stops have semi-trailers that have been retrofitted as a church. However, no one is present when one goes to the church trailers. With over three thousand

---

[1] Prepass, *Drug and Alcohol Clearinghouse*
http://prepass.com/2022/03/24/truck-driver-drugviolations-move-higher/, 12/01/2021.

truck stops in the United States, most truck stops lack a place of worship for the drivers.

Therefore, as I researched and observed the services offered at the truck stops, I realized that the churches were not present. God has blessed many churches to provide bus services for their members, but the same love was not offered to the trucking community. Most churches are in residential neighborhoods that either have truck restrictions or lack parking. Therefore, this limits a truck driver's ability to fellowship with other Christians.

As I continued observing the church's relationship with the trucking community, this idea began to resonate. *If the church supports truck drivers by conveying love and biblical ministries such as counseling, evangelism could enhance discipleship within the church body.* At this point, I prayed and sought God for directions in communicating the need for a truck stop ministry. During my Master's Program, I was led to write my Master's Thesis on the ministry. The title is *The Development of a Truck Stop Ministry; A Guide for Churches, Schools, and Students.* This document focused on the importance of the ministry, and it provided an understanding of the trucking community. This dissertation is an extension of the Master's Thesis integrating biblical counseling and addiction challenges.

The question remains, how will this project help others develop a better ministry? The world continues evolving as the church remains stagnant in some views. No longer are all people positioned in one location; many jobs require people to travel from one city or state to another. People do not follow a usual routine and regularly attend church events. However, that does not mean the same services should not be available and open in other communities.

An effective truck stop ministry can provide a learning and training experience for the church and the community. One must remember that the church is an essential part of the community. However, the community may have a business that offers services to a transit community. Therefore, some of the transit individuals may need additional assistance. These services will benefit others from within or outside the community.

A notable example is a female driver who received a phone call that her brother was on life support. Imagine being two thousand miles away from home, and the only way to return to your home location is to drive. This person is suffering from many feelings. She pulls into

8

the truck stop only to learn her brother has died. At that moment, a ministry that could help comfort her would have been beneficial.

The whole goal of the ministry is to develop a guide for the churches to use to begin a truck stop ministry and become informed about their audience. This guide will allow the churches to pray and meditate if this is a ministry for their church or the ministry would be enhanced by working with other local churches. Evangelism is essential, which can also lead to biblical counseling or coaching. One of the vital parts of coaching a person is the coach's responsibility to make the first contact.[2] Therefore, one must develop open communication skills while working at the truck stop ministry. Some of the issues one may address are death, divorce, parenting issues, mental issues, homelessness, spiritual separation, and biblical knowledge. Therefore, a trained counselor will benefit the ministry in some areas. This dissertation does not suggest that counselors should not be compensated for their work. A trained professional needs to assist in counseling sessions. However, the dissertation conveys that a well-developed ministry centered in a truck stop would offer spiritual development and growth to the truck drivers.

Declaration of the Problem

The word *declaration* is a compelling word used throughout the centuries. To provide an example of how powerful the word is, the Declaration of Independence on July 4, 1776, and this declaration announced the separation of the thirteen North American British colonies from Great Britain.[3]Declaration of Rights of Disabled Persons, which the United Nations General Assembly adopted on December 9, 1975, and on December 20, 1971, the General Assembly enhanced the declaration to include the rights of developmentally

---

[2] Gary Collins, *Christian Coaching* (Colorado Springs, CO: NavPress, 2002), 83

[3] Scott Brown, *Declaration of Independence*, Encyclopedia

Britannica, http://www.britannica.com/topic/Declaration-of-Independence, 1.

disabled persons.[4] When one researches the word declaration, the purpose is to provide hope and support to those who have been ignored or forgotten in society.

Just as the world has declared many actions to assist others, the Bible has provided declarations and decrees from God addressing His expectation of Christian life on earth. The focal Scripture of this dissertation is Luke 14:23 KJV, "And the Lord said unto the servant, Go out into the highways and byways." God made a prophetic declaration for Christians to go out into the world and seek disciples, which requires a person to help and serve others.

> This Scripture is significant in beginning any outreach ministry. God is speaking to His servants and giving directions to His expectations of Christians. The Lord told His servants to "Go." When looking at the word "go," the word means to depart from one location to another. Sometimes the ministry will remove individuals from their comfort zone and relocate them to an area of need. God expects His servant to go out into the world and encourage others to seek God.[5]

Therefore, the purpose of this dissertation is to help individuals and churches understand the importance of a truck stop ministry and begin to seek knowledge to assist those in the trucking industry.

The biblical foundation of this dissertation is based on God commanding Christians to "Go." God provided directions to many people within the Bible. Genesis 7 instructed Noah to go into the ark. God instructed Abram to go and leave the land and family and follow the path to a new land. God told Moses to go and assist in bringing the Children of Israel out of Egypt. However, in the New Testament (NT), Mark 16:15 KJV, provides specific instructions to Christians, "Go into all the world and preach the gospel to every creature." The biblical references to support this dissertation will stem from the direction in which the Bible has given many believers throughout the centuries.

---

[4] Ibid.

[5] Julie Smith, *The Development of a Truck Stop Ministry; A Guide for Churches, Schools and Students* (Charlotte, NC: Charlotte Christian College and Theological Seminary, 2021), 11.

Therefore, the truck stop ministry is not different from any other community; it is the church's responsibility to serve and continue to seek disciples. The dissertation will include additional references to the biblical foundation concerning evangelism's importance. Therefore, this aspect of the dissertation will support the ministry and open churches' eyes to recognize a need for the church in the truck stops. Since the church has not been involved in the truck stop ministry, this ministry will open the doors for churches to work together on one accord. The significant part of the truck stop ministry is that it is open to assist all individuals within the community.

Research Question and Hypothesis

Based on this dissertation's idea, if the church supports *truck drivers by conveying love and including biblical counseling, evangelism will enhance discipleship within the church body.* However, to answer the statement, one must look at the challenges one faces as a truck driver and the services not offered at the facilities. Therefore, before the researcher can provide a truthful analytical answer to the statement, one must research and understand the audience. To gain information, it is essential to complete a three-part research process while gaining knowledge.

First, the researcher will seek knowledge from counselors' writings focusing on addictions, including the importance of biblical counseling and evangelism. The truck stops are individual businesses that support the truck drivers for monetary gain.

Therefore, having a service at the truck stops based on love and support would enhance the spiritual growth of the truck drivers. The second process is to include life experiences. The researcher has obtained letters from respondents who suffer from addictions. This dissertation focuses on various addictions: drugs, obesity, gambling, the internet, and sexual desires. These addictions will be the focal dependencies for this dissertation.

These addictions were selected based on the struggles faced by some truck drivers.

The last part of the research process is to combine data obtained from the professionals in the scope of study and the life experience of the addicts. Many of the respondents have faced challenges and sought help overcoming their addiction. However, this dissertation is based on a truck stop ministry, and the information gathered proves the need for this ministry. Chapter ten will address the conclusion of the research and demonstrate written views of addicts who will provide insights into their issues and the help needed to assist them in overcoming the addiction.

Previous Research and Literature Review

The literature used for the doctoral dissertation consists of ministry training and development, teaching, counseling, addictions, and spiritual formation. This section is an overview of some of the literature used to expound on the necessity of a truck stop ministry and biblical counseling. Counseling allows a person to learn to deal with life issues while enhancing their social skills. The counselor should never try to make a counselee accept a particular approach or concept but prepare activities that will allow a person to turn their weakness into a strength. A truck stop ministry is primarily present during immediate needs that will assist a driver while away from home. So, the literature used will create a program to address primary issues while providing additional resources to continue their therapy.

To complete my Master's degree, the thesis name was *The Development of a Truck Stop Ministry*. This research aims to provide insight into the need for ministry in truck stops. Now to expand on the thesis, this dissertation will continue the research on the importance of biblical counseling in the truck stop ministry. It's essential to understand the importance of this ministry. Currently, there are no books written on the truck stop ministry. Therefore, I had to develop a book that would allow the reader to understand the ministry's needs and biblical counseling.

However, throughout the year, data has been released pertaining to the increase in drug use in the trucking community.

According to the National Library of Medicine, "the results showed a prevalence of overall drug consumption of 27.6%, particularly high consideration illicit stimulants (amphetamine consumption of 21.3% and cocaine consumption of 2.2%. It appears that truck drivers choose stimulant substances as a form of performance-enhancing drug to increase productivity.[6]

It is essential to remember that at any time, the weight of a truck can be 80,000 lbs. or more, therefore, can you imagine a person operating a commercial vehicle?

According to the National Institute of Drug Abuse, the effect of specific drugs on driving skills differs depending on how they act in the brain. For example, marijuana can slow reaction time, impair the judgment of time and distance, and decrease coordination. Drivers who have used cocaine or methamphetamine can be aggressive and reckless when driving. Certain kinds of prescription medicines, including benzodiazepines and opioids, can cause drowsiness, and dizziness and impair cognitive functioning (thinking and judgment). All of these can lead to vehicle crashes.[7]

Before understanding the cause of addiction, one must understand the function of the human body and the areas harmed by drug use. The following literature will be used to support addiction illness. *Understanding Addiction; Know Science No Stigma* by Charles Smith and Jason Hunt.[8] *Drugs, The Brain, and Behavior* by John Beck and Carlton Erickson.[9] Drug *Delivery to the Brain; Physiological Concepts, Methodologies, and Approaches* by Elizabeth De Lange and Margareta Hammarlund-Udenaes.[10]

It is essential to address the different forms of addictions—

---

[6] National Library of Medicine, *Psychoactive Drug Consumption Among Truck-Drivers: A Systematic Review of the Literature with Meta-Analysis and Meta-Regression,* ncbi.nlm.nih.gov, 2019,

8/30/2022.

[7] National Institute on Drug Abuse, Drug Driving DrugFacts, Nida.nih,gov, 01/21.2021.

[8] Chuck Smith and Jason Hunt, *Understanding Addiction Know Science, No stigma* (Visualize Publishing, 2021).

[9] John Beck and Carlton Erickson *Drugs, the Brain, and Behavior: The Pharmacology of Drug Use Disorders* (New York, NY: Routledge, 2013).

[10] Elizabeth De Lange and Margareta Hammarlund-Udenaes *Drug Delivery to the Brain: Physiological Concepts, Methodologies, and Approaches* (Switzerland: Springer, 2022).

Understanding Marijuana by Mitch Earleywine.[11] *Cocaine Addiction Theory, Research, and Treatment* by Jerome Platt deal with the long-term effects of cocaine.[12] Marijuana and cocaine addictions are two of the most used drugs of choice. These books also define the difference between cocaine and meth.

Although drugs are brain addictions, other addictions that cause damage to the brain deal with the sensory part of the brain, the literature used to support the issues related to addiction is listed below. Helping Others Overcome Addictions by Steve McVey and Mike Quarles.[13] The goal is to understand the dangers of internet addiction and the problems associated with the addiction.

The other addiction addressed in this book is body addiction. Obesity and Sexual Addictions are growing in numbers. The literature used for supporting documentation is listed below. The Sexual Desire Disorder by Helen Kaplan.[14] Your Brain on Porn: Internet Pornography and the Emerging Science of Addiction by Gary Wilson and Noah Church.[15] The Obesity Epidemic: What Caused it? How Can We Stop It? By Zoe Harcombe.[16] *The Recovery-Minded Church; Loving and Ministering to People with Addictions* by Johnathan Benz and Robb-Dover.[17]

The reader needs to understand the biblical counseling aspect of the book. The following books are used to provide supporting data

---

[11] Mitch Earleywine, *Understanding Marijuana; A New Look at the Scientific Evidence* (New York, NY: Oxford University, 2002).

[12] Jerome Platt, *Cocaine Addiction Theory, Research, and Treatment* (Boston, MA: Harvard University, 1997).

[13] Steve McVey and Mike Quarles, *Helping Others Overcome Addictions* (Eugene, OR: Harvest House, 2011.

[14] Helen Kaplan, *Sexual Desire Disorder: Dysfunctional Regulation of Sexual Motivation* (New York, NY: Brunner-Routledge, 1995).

[15] Gary Wilson and Noah Church *Your Brain on Porn: Internet Pornography and the Emerging Science of Addiction* (New York, NY: Commonwealth, 2018).

[16] Zoe Harcombe, *The Obesity Epidemic: What Caused It? How Can We Stop It?* (New York, NY: Columbus, 2010).

[17] Jonathan Benz and Kristian Robb-Dover, *The Recovery Minded Church: Loving and Ministering to People With Addiction* (Downers Grove, IL: IVP Books, 2006).

listed below. *The Moody Handbook* by Paul Enns[18]. *Quick Scripture Reference for Counseling* by John Kruis.[19] *Theory and Practices of Counseling and Psychotherapy* by Gerald Corey.[20] This research will explain that the church often has a group of people in their community that is ignored but seek healing and a relationship with God. The literature will assist the reader in the challenges of addiction and expand on the necessity of the need of the truck stop ministry supported by the churches.

Terminology

Since this dissertation will include counseling and medical terminology, the following terms are relevant to the dissertation. The goal is to provide additional knowledge and make this dissertation a tool that can be understood by all churches seeking an understanding of a truck stop ministry.

Department of Transportation is also known as the DOT. The governmental organization's purpose is to oversee and ensures that the trucking industry follows all regulation. The Department of Transportation regulates the driver's ability to drive the trucks focusing on the number of hours driven and the amount of rest a truck driver must obtain between driving shifts.

As I have previously commented, "*addiction* is a chronic disease involving substance-seeking behaviors."[21] It uses that are compulsive and hard to control despite the harmful effects when a person is addicted to a substance and is unable to function without the assistance of a counselor and treatment.

"*Drug Addiction* is a person's strong urge or craving to use a substance." Since the person cannot stop using drugs, one may develop a high tolerance level; therefore, the person needs more drugs for the same effect.

---

[18] Paul Enns, *The Moody Handbook of Theology* (Chicago, IL: Moody, 2014).

[19] John Kruis, *Quick Scripture Reference for Counseling* (Grand Rapids, MI: BakerBooks, 2013).

[20] Gerald Corey, *Theory and Practice of Counseling and Psychotherapy* (New York, NY: Cengage, 2017).

[21] Leighann Remmert and Sheila Sorrentino, *Mosby's Textbook for Nursing Assistants* (St. Louis, MO: Elsevier, 2021), 118, 718, 777. All of the following definitions are from Mosby's Textbook for Nursing Assistants

"*Alcoholism* is a liquid substance that can cause a person to become dependent upon the drink." The Bible has provided instructions on alcoholism. "And be not drunk with wine, wherein is excess, but be filled with the Spirit" (Eph. 5:18 KJV).

"*Craving* is a strong need for a drink or controlled substance." Certain actions, locations, and individuals may cause an addict to crave their drug of choice. An addict's mind begins to tell their body that the drug is needed to assist in their daily life. Although the body can survive without the drug, the addict's mind believes the drug is necessary.

Loss of control is when a person is digesting a controlled substance and is unable to reframe from taking the substance. Therefore, the person becomes addicted to the substance.[22]

"*Physical dependence* develops when a person has continued to take a controlled substance to the point they become dependent." When a person tries to stop taking the substance, their body begins to suffer from withdrawal symptoms. The symptoms can cause a traumatic reaction in the body, sometimes leading to death.[23]

"*Tolerance* is the need for more alcohol or drugs for the same effect." While each person's body is different, some individuals require a more significant substance consumption to reach the level they are attempting to achieve.

"*Drug Therapy* is when a similar drug is given to the body slowly to reduce withdrawal effects." For an individual to overcome their drug addiction, additional drugs may be needed to begin decreasing one's dependency.[24]

Opiates and other narcotics: "these drugs are strong painkillers that cause drowsiness. Some cause an intense feeling of well-being, happiness, excitement, and joy."[25]

"*Stimulants* are drugs that stimulate the brain and nervous system." When driving, stimulants can impair a person's ability to maneuver a vehicle. The stimulant will increase or reduce one's

---

[22] Ibid., 777.

[23] Ibid.

[24] Ibid.

[25] Ibid., 776.

reaction time in many situations.[26]

"*Hallucinogens* are drugs that cause sensations and images (hallucinations) that are not real. LSD is an example of a drug that affects the brain, causing a person to see images that are not present."[27]

"*Depressant*s are drugs that depress the nervous system, causing drowsiness and reduced anxiety." An example of a depressant is alcohol. Alcohol can affect a person's coordination and ability to make solid judgments.[28]

"*Marijuana* is a drug that affects the brain, causing "high. Seeing brighter colors and mood changes are common."[29] Although this drug is legal in many states, when someone abuses the drug, the drug will affect a person's ability to function.

Treatment is a long process where a person learns how to live with the cravings and ignore the need for the substance.[30] Most of the time, it is essential for a person to seek professional treatment and counseling to assist with overcoming the addiction.

"*Detoxification*, known as detox, is the process of removing a toxic substance from the body."[31]Because of the effects drugs have on a person's body. An addict may need to detox. This process can be extremely dangerous as the treatment will attempt to deprive the body of the drug. The treatment is typically completed in a medical facility to oversee this process.

"*Brain* and the spinal cord make up the nervous system."[32] The brain is connected to the spinal cord. Therefore, the brain will send signals to the nervous system, which controls a body's ability to function.

"The brain is covered by the skull. The three main parts of the brain are the cerebrum, the cerebellum, and the brainstem. The

---

[26] Ibid.

[27] Ibid.

[28] Ibid,

[29] Ibid.

[30] Ibid.

[31] Ibid.

[32] Ibid, 118

cerebrum is the largest part of the brain. The cerebellum controls the body movement, and the brain stem connects the cerebrum to the spinal cord."[33]

The Central Nervous System consists of the brain and the spinal cord. "Nerves connect to the brain, which sends messages to and from the many parts of the body.

Biblical Counseling, Wayne Mack has written biblical counseling is helping people solve their problems.[34] "It is about discovering the cause, applying biblical principles to help them overcome their problems, and giving them the necessary tools to move forward."[35]

Evangelism is communicating with others about God and encouraging others to seek salvation. Many times evangelism is conducted outside the church.

Truck Stop is a location that allows truck drivers to park during their rest period.

In most cases, the truck stop is equipped with food and basic supplies for the truck drivers.

Chapters Arrangement

Chapter two will look at the literature used to reach a conclusion of this dissertation. This chapter will focus on the primary literature used while providing examples of the benefits of the literature. The supporting data is needed to assist in proving the need for a truck stop ministry. The literature will be based on professional writers in the field whose books were not self-published and those who deal with addiction regularly. The literature used for this book is based on all forms of addiction a person may face.

Chapter three is the research methodology, one of the book's most essential parts. This section will provide the process used to prove the hypothesis of the thesis; is there a need for a truck stop ministry that includes biblical counseling? This section will give a detailed approach to providing a conclusion to the dissertation. This

---

[33] Ibid.

[34] Ibid. Wayne Mack, *A Practical Guide for Effective Biblical Counseling* (Wapwallopen, Pa: Sheppard, 2021), 27.

[35] Ibid.

dissertation will have a three-step approach. Since this dissertation focuses on biblical counseling and addictions, the first step is to layout out the information from the specialist in the area of scope. This dissertation's focus is not just on drugs but will address other addictions that affect people's ability to function.

However, others who have written about addictions have not faced addictions. Therefore, gaining a proper perspective of the control one faces while on drugs or other addictions can only be explained by those suffering from this disease. After speaking with many addicts, I obtained letters that support the struggles drivers face while suffering from addictions. The goal of obtaining the letters was to display the importance of the ministry in the truck stops.

The last step essential to the dissertation's development is the survey. I surveyed to gain a perspective on the need for a ministry in the truck stop. As the world continues to evolve, different forms of communication are necessary to reach others. One must remember the truck stop community is a group of individuals confined to a truck. Some individuals may never see again in life; however, social media and the internet are forms of communication. I took a survey that I would like to add to the dissertation. Once this data is obtained, the information will be conveyed in chapter ten of the dissertation.

Chapter four is on *evangelism*. Biblical counseling is a form of evangelism. One must understand the different approaches to counseling. This section will look at two methods, the demonological and unilateralism approach. Since many leaders often work outside the church, this section will stress the importance of ethics and moral behavior training.

Chapter five will discuss the *Effects of Drugs on the Brain and the Body*. Many addictions will affect certain parts of the body. The role of counseling someone with an addiction is to understand the damage the addiction is doing to their body. This session will provide an overview of the brain and the body focusing on the affected areas when dealing with addictions. This section is beneficial to counseling in observing red flags while in a biblical counseling session. The respondents will be used in this section to support the information obtained from the letters.

Chapter six will address *Drug Addiction*. The area will provide a brief understanding of the drugs while including respondent information. The purpose is not just to have data from a specialist but to have a human side of understanding drug addictions. Some of the respondents are also relatives of drivers and driver's children who have been drawn into the life of addiction. Although some people may have a different perspective on drug addiction, it is a disease. This chapter will also examine how a controlled substance affects one's daily functions.

Chapter seven is the addictions of *Brain Addiction*. One would say, aren't drugs a brain addiction? The answer is yes, but some addictions are not digested; some addictions are visual and stimulate the brain, causing a person to become addicted. Many drivers use gaming systems to keep them occupied. Can you imagine this time being used in the ministry? This area of the book will also address gambling.

Chapter eight will address *Body Addictions*. Body addictions will focus on obesity and sexual desires. A driver's ability to exercise is limited; therefore, it is vital to understand obesity and its effects on the body. The other section of the chapter will deal with sexual desires. One must remember this is a community of people who, in most cases, ride in a truck alone. However, this subject is sometimes limited in church discussions. This career requires a solid spiritual commitment due to the length of time many of the drivers are away from their families. This chapter will also include respondents' information about their sexual desires.

Chapter nine is *The Trucking Industry*. For one to effectively minister to another community, there needs to be an understanding of the community's standards. Most people equate truck drivers to a semi going up and down the highway; however, there is much more to the industry. Therefore, adding a chapter that would provide an overview of the industry is essential. For any ministry to be successful, the leadership must understand the audience. This section will allow the leaders to gain a background on the functionality of the industry.

Chapter ten is the conclusion, which will include the application. The section summarizes the entire dissertation, summarizing the data obtained to prove the need for a truck stop ministry. Since the research has been completed, the data demonstrated a need for biblical counseling and a ministry within the truck stop or the churches offering service to the drivers. The dissertation aims to provide information to the churches that will assist in developing effective ministries. The Bible instructed the church and

Christians to go out into the world to preach and teach the Gospel.

> According to Smith, the truck stops community has been forgotten in the religious community. How many times do individuals ride past and see hundreds of trucks parked at a truck stop? How often have you seen trucks lined on the side of the road, with men and women parking on the street with no bathroom or food options? Have you ever noticed how nicely the grocery store shelves are stocked in one's community? Truck drivers serve communities daily; however, most communities fail to acknowledge visitors within the community. Many churches are blessed with buses and vans; however, one never sees a church van at the truck stop on Sunday. While the church focuses on ministries outside the United States, this group is forgotten. How often are the United States facing hurricanes, tornados, windstorms, and pandemics? The truck drivers were out, ensuring medications, water, and food were available. Evangelism/biblical counseling is needed to encourage those in the community. Remember, most of the time, many of the drivers work alone. Imagine being alone for a week in a small truck; the church's love would help and open lines of communication with the driver. One action the earlier church did that the 21st century failed to retain they welcome visitors to their community. I'm not saying invite a stranger to your home; invite them to the church.[36]

Conclusions and Implications for Further Study

At this time, most of the research has been completed for the dissertation. The Appendix will provide the results from the respondents for the dissertation while incorporating surveys that have been completed. After collecting the letters from respondents, I have taken this data and used it to form a conclusion to the dissertation. No community should ever be excluded from the church. This book will provide insight into the trucking community.

Since there is limited information on a truck stop ministry, there is additional research that can be completed. Since the church's

---

[36] Ibid., 3.

interaction at the truck stops is limited to none, other services can be offered to the truck drivers. The goal is to reach the leaders of the churches. The book will assist the leaders in training and developing a truck stop ministry. God commands Christians to go out into the world.

Summary

Chapter one aims to provide an overview of the entire dissertation. By the end of this chapter, one should understand the purpose of this dissertation. Terminology that will be used in the project. Literature research to support the purpose of this dissertation.

Along with the information that will be provided in the additional chapters.

Chapter Two
Literature Review

The truck stop ministry is unique to the ordinary form of evangelism. Because there are limited resources relating to the development of this outreach ministry, the literature used combined integrated sources, displaying the needs of the trucking community. Therefore, to complete the research for this dissertation, a four-part process was necessary to convey the spiritual need for the church's presence at the truck stops. The question posed in this dissertation is biblical counseling dealing with addictions and the need for a truck stop ministry. Therefore, the areas the dissertation will focus on are the biblical foundation, development of the truck stop ministry, counseling, and addictions.

Biblical Foundation

When answering the question of whether a ministry is needed in a truck stop that offers counseling services, a researcher must look at the biblical examples God provided. Leaders will never have a successful ministry unless they seek God first for directions.

The focal Scripture for this dissertation looks at the truth and guidance God has given all Christians. Luke 14:23 has many translations; however, the Living Bible provides a deep understanding of God's commandments and supports this dissertation. "Go out into the country lanes and behind the hedges and urge anyone you find to come so that the house will be full" (Luke 14:23). This Scripture has an essential action word/verb God used to command all Christians. God commands Christians to "go." However, this translation states for one to go behind the hedges. Every event for evangelism is not always right in front of an individual. Sometimes one must go to places that may be forgotten to seek disciples. A truck stop ministry is a group of individuals who have been forgotten.

According to the Webster Online Dictionary, the word go has the following definitions: to proceed, to travel to a place, to travel to and say in a place for a while, and to leave and depart.[1] Evangelism is

---

[1]Webster Dictionary, https://www.merriam-

a critical part of any ministry. Just as Jesus traveled from community to community spreading the Gospel, God expects Christians to display the same love within their communities. Chapter four will provide additional insight into evangelism. It is essential that when a leader goes into the community, sometimes there are unique places one will visit while on their disciple-making journey.

Paul provides a great example of the character of a leader when working in the ministry. Philippians 1:1-7 displays the love and compassion needed when working in a ministry. Paul expressed his love for God; in any ministry, love is essential to reach others. Paul was humble, understanding his ministry's position as a servant of God. *Pastoral Ministry According to Paul, A Bible Vision* by James W. Thompson provides leadership overviews using the historical foundation based on Paul and his relationship and passion for God.[2] This book offers an excellent reference to the characteristics of Paul and how Christians must act during evangelism. Jensen's Survey of the Old Testament by Irving Jenson[3] *and Jensen's Survey of the New Testament* by Irving Jensen provided the surveyed research needed to support the dissertation based on the historical foundation.[4] Jensen's surveys of both the Old and New Testaments looks at the historical context of the chapters and provide an overview of the biblical references.

Development of the Ministry

One must remember that counseling allows one to learn to deal with life issues while enhancing social skills. The counselee should never be forced to accept a particular approach or concept but prepare activities that will allow a person to turn their weakness into a strength. The goal of this ministry is to assist a transit community while working

---

webster/com/dictionary/go?src=search-dict-box, 2022, 9/1/2022.

[2] James Thompson, *Pastoral Ministry According to Paul: A Biblical Vision* (Grand Rapid, MI: Baker Academic, 2006).

[3] Irving Jersen, *Jensen's Survey of the Old Testament: Search and Discover* (Chicago, IL: Moody,1978).

[4] *Irving Jensen, Jensen's Survey of the New Testament* (Chicago, IL: Moody, 1977).

in other areas. The churches should welcome truck drivers; therefore, providing the literature used will help develop and answer the question posed by the dissertation. Is a truck stop ministry needed?

To complete my Master's degree, my thesis was *The Development of a Truck Stop Ministry*.

> This book aims to teach others about the need for a truck stop ministry. In the beginning, most people did not have a proper industry perspective. The sacrifices these men and women provide are unbelievable. Before beginning this industry study, many stereotypes surround the industry, and to be honest, and some are nervous because of the comments. However, as an individual travels throughout the United States and stops at rest areas and travel centers, something is missing. Where are the churches? Why are there no church representatives present? This trucking community appears to be forgotten.[5]

This research aims to provide insight into the need for ministry in truck stops. Since this is an expansion of the Master's Thesis, this book will include the challenges of addiction when working as a truck driver. This dissertation does not state that all drivers suffer from addictions; however, a ministry that can assist those suffering from an addiction would benefit the drivers' spiritual growth. Now to expand on the thesis, no books on record discussing the development of a truck stop ministry. Therefore, it was essential to utilize literature that assisted in building the ministry.

Literature on Addiction

As stated in the introduction, before understanding the cause of addiction, one must understand the function of the human body and the areas harmed by drug use. The following literature will be used to support addiction illness. *Understanding Addiction; Know Science No Stigma* by Charles Smith and Jason Hunt provides insights into the actions' reason.[6] The information in this book is essential in

---

[5] Ibid., 8.

[6] Chuck Smith and Jason Hunt. *Understanding Addiction, Know Science, No Stigma* (Visual, 2021).

understanding that addiction is a disorder that is not different from any other disease a person may face. Like all other diseases, seeking help and proper treatment is essential.

Drugs, The Brain, and Behavior by John Beck and Carlton Erickson provides an understanding of how drugs affect the brain's functionality.[7] Before a person induces a change in their life, one must become mindful of that which is controlling them. The author focuses on the human mind and how one must change their configuration of thought to overcome the challenges faced by addictions. Until a person is willing to introduce change in their life, healing will not begin. Therefore, this audiotape discusses the emotional challenges within the mind.

Drug Delivery to the Brain; Physiological Concepts, Methodologies, and Approaches by Elizabeth De Lange help one understand the effects of drugs, including gaining a perspective on how drugs reach the brain after being introduced to the body. This book provides a group of professionals specializing in brain-drug delivery. It is essential to gain professional opinions as well as addicts. It offers a variety of viewpoints that will assist in understanding the brain's functions and the effect of the chemical in a body's blood supply.[8]

It is essential to address the different forms of addictions. *Understanding Marijuana* by Mitch Earleywine provides the history of marijuana. In many states, marijuana has been legalized.[9] However, this plant is known for having healing properties for many elements. However, one must look at a drug's effects when abused. All drug has a dosage to assist in healing without causing substantial harm to a person's ability to function. This book will provide an understanding of the drug and support the data within the dissertation.

Dr. Earleywine obtained a Ph.D. in 1968 and joined the psychology department faculty at the University of Wisconsin the

[7] John Beck and Carlton Erickson *Drugs, the Brain, and Behavior: The Pharmacology of Drug Use Disorders* (New York, NY: Routledge, 2013).

[8] Elizabeth C. M. DeLange and Margaret Hammerlund-Udenaes, Robert G. Throne *Drug Delivery to the Brain, Physiological Concepts, Methodologies, and Approaches* (San Francisco, CA: Springer, 2014), ix.

[9] Mitch Earleywine, *Understanding Marijuana; A New Look at the Scientific Evidence* (New York, NY: Oxford University, 2002).

following year; Marijuana use had reached an all-time high.[10] Due to Earleywine's prior marijuana research, Earleywine continued his research by joining the University of Washington in 1970.[11] "I extended my research in cognitive and social determinants of alcohol use to the study of marijuana effect on humans.[12] "Earleywine deserves considerable credit for his ability to provide a comprehensive and scientifically objective review of this continuously controversial topic in *Understanding Marijuana.*[13]

Cocaine Addiction Theory, Research, and Treatment by Jerome Platt is an audiobook that deals with the long-term effects of cocaine.[14] To face rehabilitation, one must understand the damage cocaine does to the body. One of the phrases in the audio resonates with the importance of seeking the facts about one's drug of choice.

If you decide to fight the cocaine demon or want to help a loved one beat their addiction, you must educate yourself on how cocaine affects the brain.

Understanding why it is nearly impossible to fight the addiction on your own and why you need medical intervention is critical so that you can save your own life or the life of a loved one using.[15]

Although drugs are brain additions, other addictions that cause damage to the brain deal with the sensory part of the brain, the literature used to support the issues related to addiction. *Internet Addiction: Helping Others Overcome Addictions* by Steve McVey and Mike Quarles looks at the problems of internet addiction. "But as I've directed a recovery ministry for the last 16 years. I have observed that it follows that people find freedom when they are confronted with the truth. There must be an encounter with Christ and a revelation of the Holy Spirit."[16] The goal is to understand the dangers of internet

---

[10] Ibid., vi.

[11] Ibid.

[12] Ibid.

[13] Ibid.

[14] Jerome Platt, Cocaine Addiction Theory, Research, and Treatment (Boston, MA: Harvard University, 1997).

[15] Ibid., 15.

[16] Ibid., 15.

addiction and the problems associated with the addiction.

The other addiction addressed in this book is body addiction. Obesity and sexual addictions are growing in numbers. The literature used for supporting documentation is listed below. *The Sexual Desire Disorder* by Helen Kaplan looks at the issues associated with sexuality. According to Kaplan, almost two decades have passed since I first described the syndrome of hypoactive sexual desires and suggested that disorders of sexual desire constitute distinct clinical entities that are different from, and on a par with, erectile and orgasm phase dysfunctions.[17] *Your Brain on Porn: Internet Pornography and the Emerging Science of Addiction* by Gary Wilson and Noah Church.[18] Understanding the issues of porn addiction is essential for a truck stop ministry. *The Obesity Epidemic: What Caused it? How Can We Stop It?* by Zoe Harcombe.[19] Harcombe provided a book on why people face obesity and training on improving one's nutrient health. *The Recovery-Minded Church, Loving and Ministering to People with Addictions* by Johnathan Benz and Robb-Dover will assist in understanding the need for churches that help others overcome addictions. "So, this book is for those who dream of a prodigal future for their church and seek the tools for their own spiritual transformation in the form of a vibrant, radically loving relationship with the addicts in their pews and just outside their doors,[20]

The reader needs to understand the biblical counseling aspect of the book. The following books provide supporting data listed below. *The Moody Handbook* by Paul Enns offers an understanding of biblical theories.[21] One must understand how addictions affect people's ability to battle addictions. Enns defines the theories to assist others with gaining a perspective of biblical references. Quick

---

[17] Helen Kaplan, *The Sexual Desire Disorders Dysfunctional Regulation of Sexual Motivation* (New York, NY: Routledge, 2015), 1.

[18] Gary Wilson, Noah Church *Your Brain on Porn: Internet Pornography and the Emerging Science of Addiction* (New York, NY: Commonwealth, 2018).

[19] Zoe Harcombe, *The Obesity Epidemic: What Caused It? How Can We Stop It?* (New York, NY: Columbus, 2010).

[20] Jonathan Benz and Kristina Robb-Dover, *The Recovery-Minded Church Loving and Ministering to People with Addictions* (Downers Grove, IL: IVP Books, 2018), 11.

[21] Paul Enns, *The Moody Handbook of Theology* (Chicago, IL: Moody, 2014).

Scripture Reference for Counseling by John Kruis provided a tool that can be used during a biblical counseling session.[22] Kruis used Scriptures and categorized them to deal with many issues. For the dissertation, this book will assist in the utilization of scriptures to support the data within the dissertation. Theory and Practices of Counseling and Psychotherapy by Gerald Corey provides an understanding of therapy techniques.

The major strength of this theory is that it identifies with dysfunctional thinking. This type of counseling requires a client to learn problem-solving. Behavior changes involve the therapist and counselee working together, sometimes engaging in sarcastic dialogue. The theory assists the client in developing skills to retain the progress made during the counseling session. To reach this point, a person remains open to change while completing the assignment and strengthening their thinking.[23]

In any counseling session, communication is essential. The truck stop is a diverse community; therefore, gaining a perspective of learning styles is vital. It is crucial to develop skills that will assist a person in communicating effectively in biblical counseling.

Summary

This research will seek to provide facts that the church often has a group of people in their community that is ignored but seek healing and a relationship with God. The literature will assist the reader in the addiction challenges and expand on the necessity of the need for truck stop ministry supported by the churches. The purpose of this material is to assist the church community in understanding biblical counseling and references to assist in the ministry. The truck stop is a community of multiple cultures. Therefore, the goal is to help those with addiction seek the truth and learn to deal with their struggles. The

---

[22] John Kruis, Quick Scripture Reference for Counseling (Grand Rapids, MI: BakerBooks, 2013).

[23] Gerald Corey, Theory and Practice of Counseling and Psychotherapy (India: Cengage, 2013). 285.

literature combined will provide a process and express the importance of a truck stop ministry. Upon the completion of this chapter, the reader should have an understanding of the literature that will be offered in the dissertation to support the writings.

Chapter Three
Research Methodologies

This chapter is one of the most critical chapters in the book. It is essential to understand the reasoning and research completed to come to a conclusion that answers the dissertation's research question. As stated before, the research question is, *is biblical counseling needed in the development of a truck stop ministry?* The church has been present in the world for centuries; therefore, one may ask why a ministry needs to be developed. This chapter will discuss the ministry and the need for Christians to serve at the truck stops.

Gathering pertinent information and data is essential to provide a detailed understanding of the ministry. Chapter two provided a group of professionals who have specialized in counseling and biblical counseling. However, although many people can provide information about the ministry, counseling, and addiction, only those living with this disease can communicate the effects of addictions and their personal experiences.

Therefore, this dissertation will combine the information from the specialist and those suffering from addiction. The goal is to look at many drivers' struggles and how a biblical counseling ministry would assist in the driver's spiritual growth and healing.

When A Loved One Dies

As I thought about the issues many truck drivers face, I thought it would be essential to elaborate on chapter one's overview, which is a true story to begin this portion of the dissertation. A female truck driver was working in California; when she received an extremely distressing phone call. At the time, she did not know the full scope of the issue; the only message she understood was that her younger brother was in the hospital on life support. Imagine the confusion and despair knowing that her brother had been placed on life support and she was in California.

Immediately, she contacted her dispatch and canceled any loads that were not going to her brother's location. Finally, dispatch sent a route that would get her to her brother. As she sat and thought about the situation, the only thing that resonated in her mind was, what happened? How could the baby of the family be this ill? She began to drive, remaining focused on the road but caught her mind still wondering and pondering about the situation. Although she prayed, her heart was still heavy with sorrow.

She pulled over to a truck stop to fuel the truck. When she checked her phone for an update, she was sent a picture of her brother in the hospital. Viewing this picture and being thousands of miles away from home was devastating. As she saw her brother lying in the hospital bed with saline intravenously provided to her brother, and breathing tube, and additional medical equipment, she knew she had to get to the hospital. She sat at the truck stop for a while to gain her composure and continued her journey to the hospital.

This journey seemed to be never-ending. There was nothing she could do but pray and drive.

While she was driving, she received a phone call from a relative. The message relayed was that the doctors wanted to meet with the family. Anyone who has worked in the healthcare field or has dealt with a death in the hospital knows that when a doctor asks to speak with the family, a decision must be made. As she continued to drive, her nerves were taking over, and finally, she had to let someone else drive the truck. No longer was it safe for her to drive in that condition. Therefore, she sat and waited for the conference call with the doctor.

Finally, the conference call began. The doctors explained that her brother had little to no brain activity, and his organs were starting to shut down. As the family asked many questions to see what options were available, the doctor stated there was no hope and suggested that the family remove him from life support. However, the siblings could not make the decision, only his son. As she sat and listened, she prayed that God would provide his son with the wisdom needed to make the correct decision. The son said, how can I determine when a person should live or die? Therefore, I do not wish for my father to be removed from life support.

As she sat there, she was thankful that he had decided not to end her brother's life.

The feeling of hope began to overtake her heart. She still had time to get to her brother; maybe God would heal him. However, it was his time to go home. At 3 am, his blood pressure began to drop. The family notified her and asked how far away she was from the hospital. She was approximately five hundred miles away from the hospital. However, she remained on the path, believing she would arrive and see her brother.

Once more, she stopped for fuel and called the family, only to find out that he had just passed. At that point, there was no longer a sense of urgency to drive. She went to the restaurant and sat down and cried. The pain was heartbreaking, and as people tried to comfort her, she was still distressed. Three hours later, her brother was still in the room when she arrived at the hospital. Watching the baby lying in bed, never smiling or speaking again, was difficult. As I stated, this was a true story. The only part I reframed to say is that I was the one who experienced this loss. As stated before, I stopped at different truck stops throughout the journey. Having a professional counselor to share the experience with would have helped while coping with death.

This project has been ongoing for five years. Since my brother died of an overdose, I felt it was necessary to learn more about addictions so that maybe the ministry could save one person from drug addiction. Therefore, this project will consist of a two-part evaluation process. Understanding the effects of addiction should not be just the information found in a book. Consequently, I needed to reach out and obtain respondents that would provide their stories. The goal is to give a human side to the addiction by comparing the data from the books and relating it to the emotions and struggles faced by the addiction.

Considering truck driving requires most drivers to be alone. Without the power of God, many drivers become addicted to one of these actions. Therefore, a letter was provided to individuals who suffer from addictions and the children of an addict. The letter's purpose was to seek approval for the individuals willing to discuss their stories.

Since a trained counselor was not available to assist with individual counseling sessions, each respondent was asked to write about their experiences dealing with addiction.

According to Corey, when engaging in any communication that could be perceived as counseling, it's crucial to provide a document that adds clarity and expectations of the project.[1]

This consent form provided the respondent with the purpose of the study to collect data and determine if a truck stop ministry is needed in the truck stops, which includes biblical counseling. Appendix one provides an example of the form we sent to each respondent. It provides procedures assisting the respondent and defining the scope of the project. The value of the project is that it allows people to communicate in writing when the struggle may be too difficult to discuss. Confidentiality is essential when working with others, especially with individuals struggling with addictions—lastly, the person signs giving one permission to utilize their information. Once the consent form was returned, many of the respondents began to submit their stories immediately.

The evaluation process will include true life stories compared

---

[1] Gerald Corey, Theory and Practice of Counseling and Psychotherapy (India: Cengage, 2013) 274.

to the printed data. An example is looking at the life story of the respondent. While reading the information, compare and determine which psychotherapy concepts would be the most beneficial while including what type of addiction the person is facing. This evaluation process provides data on drivers' struggles with drug addiction or other addictions. The goal is to display the truck ministry's needs and biblical counseling. The first part consists of the stories of the respondents, and the second part will correlate the actions of the drivers with the data of the specialist focusing on examples of why biblical counseling should be at the truck stops.

Respondent One

When I was first asked to write about my experience growing up with an addict in the household, the first thing that popped into my mind was a conversation I had with a man who was 50 years old and a former addict. I was 14 years old, and my mother was the subject of my experience. One day this man, who was my mother's sugar daddy since before I could walk, picked me up from school as requested by my mother and began to inquire about my wellbeing. Sometime during that conversation, I started complaining about the care I was receiving as my mother's son. I told him that even though I've always felt loved by my mother, I didn't think she did what other kids' mothers did. She never took me anywhere; she never attended any PTA meetings. I would always go without things that most people wouldn't even consider. I was never registered for school, got shots on time, and my clothes were not cleaned unless I cleaned them. I learned early to cook for myself; anything she fed me was fast food. As I got older, I would say she loved me; she was not the mother type. This much older former addict tried to help me. She looked me right in the eye and told me one of the most factual statements that anyone had ever spoken to me. He said, "Son, I need you to understand something very well. Your mother loves you, but nothing comes before the drugs." At the time, I was angry and insulted. I can honestly say my feelings were hurt by the unfiltered truth that I wasn't ready to hear. He told me that the drugs would talk to her, tell her what to think, and control her mind. He told me it was the most crucial thing in his life when he got high. It came before everything, and it took him three heart attacks and months in the hospital to finally walk away from the drugs. I can say with confidence that he was 100% correct. I have a very loving mother. We have a great relationship. She's more like a mother friend. I've always been able to talk to her about anything, no matter how personal or embarrassing. And I remember thinking I could convince her to become a normal mother free from drugs. And I tried repeatedly.

I always knew when she was getting high. She would lock herself in the bathroom for hours at a time to have peace while she would get high. I found that to be a perfect time to shame her. I would be right next to the bathroom door, blowing her high. I'd preach to her for hours about how she was affecting her children's lives by choosing drugs over us and robbing us of a normal upbringing. I would be the voice of reason to a mind detached from reality. I would take every opportunity to let her know we would never have an everyday life because of her decisions. It was far from ordinary life because of my mother's decisions. I've seen and been through some genuinely abnormal situations.

Before I was 18, I witnessed people beaten in the streets; two men were shot and left bleeding on my porch, and my house was robbed on more than a few occasions. I watched my cousin suffer from paranoid delusions and later overdose in my kitchen while I stood beside her. I watched a man knock a guy out in my basement and later knock himself out. I witnessed a guy stripping out of his clothes in my bathroom while screaming, "They're everywhere!" Though he was covered with bugs when none were there. I witnessed a man wrestling with a folding metal chair, believing a group of strangers was attacking him. The police raided my house on four different occasions. It got to the point that I no longer freaked out when the police broke down my front door with guns out, telling everybody to get on the ground. People have been stabbed, beaten, and threatened with firearms in the head where I grew up. I can trace it all back to drugs because addicts bring baggage.

They have addicts, drug dealers, and thug friends who always want company. Since I was 12, I have been kicking out adults from my mother's house. A few of them were very dangerous. I learned the art of diplomacy, finesse, and aggression from dealing with extreme personalities. My mother habitually allowed homeless underage girls into our home throughout the years. I find that unique to addicts because she would allow the girls to stay in our home indefinitely. She always had a good heart that way, but no average person of ordinary mind would allow strangers around their children. Then there are the legal problems of an addict.

My mother has been arrested on multiple occasions. Visits to cook county jail were a regular thing for me. A few times, she made it to the prison. I remember getting a call from a former neighbor of mine informing me that my mother was fighting with a police officer and being arrested right before her. My mother had a habit of running. She ran out of a court building when she was sentenced to jail. Once I was taking the trash out and placing the garbage in the can, she sped up the alley doing about 70 MPH right in front of me; about three police cars followed three seconds later. She got away that day. When I saw her late that night and asked what it was about, she said they tried to pull her over, and she had drugs in the car, so she ran. That wasn't the first high-speed chase that happened.

I've had many experiences that were far from ordinary and directly resulted from my mother's drug abuse. The one thing that shines through the madness is that the drugs come first. They always have. Maybe one day, that'll change. I'm reminded of the study where a researcher gave a mouse a choice between cocaine and food and starved to death. No amount of love, shaming, pleading, begging, or bribing can change an addict.

Being a truck driver requires me to have a random drug test. However, I found myself choosing a drug of choice: marijuana. However, I asked myself why I even considered doing drugs when I witnessed it as a child. Being on the road alone is a challenge sometimes. I love being with my family; however, I know the importance of supporting my family. Having a group or organization present at the truck stop would help when I needed to use drugs. At the beginning of the year, I realized I needed to change my life. I stopped using marijuana.

Comments And Supporting Data for Respondent One

It's essential for parents and guardians of children to be aware of actions within one's home and how they can affect children. Proverbs 22:6 reminds parents of their responsibility when raising children: to train a child in the word of God. Since Respondent One grew up in a household where drugs were used, he was forced to learn right from wrong. The cognitive behavior approach is essential to help Respondent One deal with his addiction. "Cognitive restructuring involves teaching clients to me be more aware of their negative thoughts, to evaluate evidence of the extent to which their thoughts are accurate, and to replace unrealistic thoughts with more-balanced interpretations, predictions, and assumptions."[2] Although Respondent One engaged in drug activity, they learned to reframe from the cravings for drugs. This Respondent supports the need for a truck stop ministry. While Respondent One was dealing with the cravings for marijuana and working as a truck driver, having a ministry present would have provided guidance in his need for change and helped him deal with his childhood experiences.

Respondent Two

So, if you want to start and go backward, my story is that I have six months into operating my authority and being a hotshot driver. The Lord has given me this opportunity through investors and a loan from my mom's trust. The Lord is active in my life, and I wish I had more of a place to go at truck stops. I've seen two truck chapels in the hundreds that I have visited. The way these chapels are presented has made me feel very intimidated, and there were no signs saying welcome come on in or anything, so it was daunting to walk in the door not knowing what was on the other side. Therefore, the need for a truck ministry is needed. Being a truck driver, God teaches me daily to trust in him. Despite all my struggles, he always provides a way out. Just like Jesus says in life, he doesn't always take away all the efforts and trials that come your way but always provides a way out. You may not see it until later, or you may see it right away, but through it all, through the trials and tribulations, through the truck breakdowns and the tire blowouts, God is teaching me that he is here at every step of the way he is holding my hand even when I feel like he's not. I think having a welcoming presence would be awesome for truckers because they struggle as I work daily with all the stresses of trucking, which is becoming a very stressful profession for me. And if someone could reach just a few through prayer, I think the trucking ministry could significantly impact truck stops. Those willing to take that risk and ask

---

[2] Ibid., 275.

for prayer or to walk in and have fellowship with another Christian, I know I feel very alone most of the time. I don't have many family members or friends, so when I meet somebody like Julie, it is refreshing to talk to someone with experience in the trucking industry—to communicate with someone who can answer questions and share the love of the Lord and a heart for people.

I have been clean and sober for over three years, and I feel like trucking gets addicts away from their environment. Being a truck driver allows me to go out on the road and focus on other things besides drugs. In the realm of things, drug addicts always know where to find drugs. But having a profession that does not focus on drugs and is not easily found among truckers is a ministry. I think it would significantly improve the recovery and the number of relapses drug addicts face.

Especially with the money a truck driver begins to make, they start seeing how trucking can change their lives, get them out of their immediate environment, and provide an opportunity to meet successful people. The motivating factor for me is that relapse could jeopardize all one has worked for as a business owner. Trucking ministry would benefit those in recovery, either from alcohol or drugs, because it becomes lonely in the truck stops. It would be a pleasant refuge for those struggling with loneliness, addiction, and other things. Also, I think it would be a great place where truckers could converse and get information about loads of different jobs, just everything about trucking, and in a positive, Godly environment.

Comments and Support Data for Respondent Two

The first time I met Respondent Two, Respondent Two was walking in the truck stop parking lot. I had noticed them several times, and Respondent Two approached me when I left my truck. After engaging in a conversation, Respondent Two appeared to need someone to communicate with or listen to. At the time, I did not understand Respondent Two's issues. However, I continued to listen.

Christian Counseling, written by Gary Collins, is defined as an excellent example of the feeling of loneliness.

"Loneliness is a painful inner emptiness that everybody experiences at times. It may last for a short time or persist throughout life. It impacts people of all ages, including early childhood, but it appears to grow during the teenage years and may reach its highest peak in young adults in their early twenties. Although it appears in all cultures, it is most prevalent in societies that emphasize individualism. It frequently occurs in single adults living alone, elderly people who have lost a spouse, parents without partners, or people away from home, including students. It can characterize people who live apart from other human beings, but it is possible to be lonely and surrounded by other people."[3]

As I sat and continued to listen to the conversation, Respondent Two began to discuss their drug addiction. I realize Respondent Two was dealing with a serious drug addiction; however, as I spoke with her, I realized she needed someone to convey her challenges to and provide hope. Therefore, during this conversation, I asked if having a truck stop ministry would benefit one's recovery. Respondent Two felt it would be helpful for her and others who face the same struggles. The ministry would help with the addiction and the loneliness one feels while struggling.

Addiction continues to affect many people in the world. According to Collins, addiction is one of the significant issues in the world. Since this addiction continues to plague society, it is essential to have trained professionals to assist in helping people through their recovery. The information from Respondent Two supports that a truck stop ministry is needed at the truck stops. Luke 14:23 is this dissertation's focal scripture, reminding Christians that sometimes one must go outside the church and help others.

Respondent Three

My first experience gaining knowledge about drug abuse began when I worked as a Foster Care Case Manager. I worked with children in Child Protective Services custody. During my time as a foster care caseworker, in approximately 90% of my cases, the children were removed from their parent's control due to parental drug abuse. I never

---

[3] Gary Collins, Christian Coaching (Colorado Springs, CO: NavPress, 2002), 195.

knew anyone personally who struggled with addiction until I began dating Oliver. I started dating Oliver in November 2016. During our first conversation, he informed me that God had delivered him from drugs many years earlier. He was open and honest about it from the beginning. As our relationship progressed, he repeatedly said he was "one bad decision away" from relapsing. I thought that was his way of saying he was careful about decision-making. We dated long-distance for several months before he moved to where I live.

The first time Oliver admitted to using drugs to me was in the summer of 2018. He traveled to his home state for a month to visit his family. I noticed that Oliver did not call me very much; two or more days would go by before I would hear from him, but I attributed that to him being busy catching up with family and friends. When he did contact me, he sounded normal but asked for money. Thinking nothing of it, I sent him money because Oliver was struggling financially, and I assumed Oliver was running short because Oliver was spending time with family, friends, and grandchildren.

One day, he called me in a panic, asking for $50.00. He stated that "someone had taken his car," and he needed $50.00 to get it back. Scared, I asked what was happening and if he had been mugged. He stated that he had "gone around the wrong people" and was drinking and "lost control," and he did some drugs. He further said he needed $50.00 to get the car back and some gas money to get back to Texas. I don't remember how much money I sent Oliver, probably around $200.00. When he returned, I remember him sending some cash to someone back in his home state. When I asked what that was all about, he said it was an "old drug debt." I didn't question him; I just left it alone, thinking it was an isolated incident because everyone could make a mistake.

The next time Oliver used drugs was in July 2019, though I have no proof. But he exhibited the same behavior in the summer of 2018. Oliver left for an extended visit to his home state. He drove home; once he arrived, he asked me for some money for food. He was staying with his brother and stated that his brother had little food in the home. I sent him money. Once again, two to three days would go by before I would receive a phone call from him, but each time he did, he needed money.

Again, he was still not making much money and was looking for a job. Oliver worked at one of the public schools in Texas. He had completed the school year in a school district and was not returning. He was still being paid, thru the end of August 2019, as his contract would end on September 1, 2019. At one point, almost one week went by without me hearing from him. I called him but got no answer. I reached out to his daughter to see if she could get ahold of Oliver for me. I never heard back from her, but Oliver texted me via Facebook. He told me that his phone bill was due, and his phone would only accept incoming calls and texts. He was not able to text back or make calls. However, he could use his brother's Wi-Fi to contact me via Facebook. He said he needed money to get home. Again, knowing that he did not make a lot of money, I sent him money to get home, and I also paid his telephone bill so he would have a phone while traveling. I remember that I was leaving for Arkansas for a conference the same day Oliver would be coming home. We met at a gas station in Arkansas. I filled Oliver's gas tank, gave him a few extra dollars, and ate lunch together. He seemed fine and acted normal.

We discussed our trips when I returned home from the conference a few days later. As we talked, I asked Oliver how he enjoyed the events he attended when he visited home. To my surprise, he said he didn't do most of what he had planned. When I asked why he said due to lack of money; I was a bit surprised since I had sent him money and he had money before he left. I did mention to him that we were too far along in our relationship for him to be out of contact with me for several days; after that conversation, everything appeared normal.

The year 2020 changed not only my life, but everyone's in society. Covid-19 hit, and Oliver and I were stuck at home all year. As a teacher, I taught the remainder of the school year and summer school online. Oliver was a Teacher Paraprofessional. He continued to get paid, but there was no work for him to do, being that he was a Teacher's Assistant. We went nowhere other than to the store and back home. Oliver's friend and his wife visited in May 2020. I remember that, during this visit, Oliver and his friend went to the home of their best friend's father-in-law. I thought they were going to visit. The following March 2021, I found out that this individual had cocaine, and they bought some. His friend informed me they did cocaine in the garage, which was why they could stay up all night during his visit.

But after the next trip to his home state, in March 2021, I got an actual perspective of Oliver's drug use. The next trip that Oliver made home was a disaster. After this trip, his good friend told me the truth and that he was still using drugs. In March 2021, Oliver went to his home state to participate in a ministry activity at his former church. The week of March 15th was spring break in Texas. Oliver left on March 12th to head to his home state; the plan was for him to be there the following week for practices (with the ministry). He would participate in the ministry on March 21st. The plan was to leave immediately after and drive for a few hours. He would stay somewhere overnight, then finish the drive back to Texas on March 22, 2021; due to Oliver's work schedule, Oliver was scheduled to return to work on March 23, 2021. Oliver arrived in his home state on March 13th. He kept in touch with me on March 13th and 14th. I did not hear from him on March 15th, but he called me on March 16th, and we talked. He sounded normal and said he had been busy visiting family and friends and preparing for ministry. A few days went by without hearing from him. We talked sometime around March 17th or so. During this conversation, he informed me that his best friend's wife had passed, and we would travel to Oklahoma the following week to attend the funeral.

After this conversation, a few days passed without me hearing from him. I texted him on March 20th, stating that I was concerned because I had not heard from him. On March 21st, I contacted Oliver to send him well wishes for his ministry that evening. He informed me that he might need cash to get home. He stated that he had not received his stimulus check (which was odd because I had). I told him I would send him cash the next day after work. On March 22nd, I sent him $250.00. He was scheduled to leave Illinois on March 21 and should have been well on his way back to Texas. Oliver stated he was exhausted from ministry and would leave on March 23rd. I did not hear anymore from him on March 22nd. On March 23rd, I texted him early in the morning and asked if he was on the road home. He said "no" and that he was having a car problem. He said the car was not going into gear, and the transmission was slipping. However, he had the car checked before he left; oil change and brakes.

Later that day, he said he could have the car fixed, but it would cost him $500.00; I sent the money. However, Oliver never responded that he had received the money. I did not hear from him anymore that day. I texted again on March 24th. Oliver said the car would be ready that afternoon, and he would head back to Texas. We discussed the plans for getting to Oklahoma on Friday. I heard no more from Oliver that day, March 24th. On March 25th, I texted Oliver early in the morning. He informed me that he was waiting in the car outside his ex-mother-in-law's home to borrow gas money from his daughter. At this point, I got angry because I had sent him over $700.00 over the last few days for the car repair and to get home. I reminded Oliver that he could use his credit cards for gas, as he had told me he had "plenty of credit buying power." He said he did not bring all his credit cards and needed to save the credit card to get a hotel room. Later that day, March 25th, I sent him another $250.00. He said he was leaving right after he picked up the money.

He texted at 5:30 pm and said he had the money and was "on his way." Oliver called on March 25th, late in the evening, and said he would drive all night to get back then we would leave for Oklahoma Friday evening. He stated he was in Missouri at the time. I heard nothing from Oliver on Friday, March 26th, and he did not arrive home. On Saturday, March 27th, I began calling and texting early in the morning. I did not get ahold of him until March 27th at 7 am. He was incoherent and kept falling asleep on the phone. I continued to call, and he kept falling asleep, saying he needed to get his bearings.

By this time, I was furious. I yelled at Oliver and hung up. I did not hear from him all that day when we were supposed to be in Oklahoma for his friend's wife's funeral. After not hearing from Oliver on March 27th, nor did he return home. I reached out to his friend Sebastian hoping Oliver had detoured to Oklahoma for the funeral. After speaking with Sebastian, I was even angrier. Sebastian said he had not heard from Oliver, nor did he attend the funeral. I told Sebastian how I had sent him money and the car issues. Sebastian was disturbed to find out that Oliver had not returned to Texas since leaving on March 12th.

Sebastian said Oliver was probably on something and called him; I did not understand that terminology (later, I found out this meant he was on drugs). Sebastian called me back and said that he had talked to Oliver and that his phone was off, meaning he could only accept incoming calls and texts and could not return/make calls or place texts. Olive was somewhere in Arkansas. Sebastian said he had a firm conversation with Oliver about his behavior.

When I called Oliver back, I gave him my debit card number so he could pay his phone bill. I didn't want him on the road without a working phone. I questioned him repeatedly about where he had been and why he was not staying in touch with me regarding his whereabouts. Oliver said he was trying to "do too much" and did not sleep enough. He said he was trying to drive back without much sleep, fell asleep, and drove his car into a ditch. Therefore, Oliver had to use a credit card to pay to get the car out of the ditch. Oliver said he did not want to tell me because he knew I would worry. I told him I was angry that Oliver was not keeping in touch with me; Oliver apologized and stated he would be home that evening. After leaving on March 12th, he returned on the evening of March 29th. During this ordeal, I felt in my gut that Oliver had done drugs and was afraid to tell me. I was just glad he was home. Little did I know my suspicions would be confirmed the next day.

Out of the blue, on March 29, 2021, I received a message from Oliver's good friend Robert. He asked me if Oliver had made it home. I told him yes and that I was in a panic because he had had one problem after another; then, I could not get ahold of him for a few days. Robert then said, "We all worry when he goes home." I told him that I understood and that it is challenging to live out of town, then go home because you wear yourself out trying to visit everyone. Robert advised me I should go with him the next time Oliver went home. Then he asked how Oliver looked. I said, "tired and frustrated." Robert stated that he knew things that I did not. I told him that if he was referring to Oliver's past drug use, I was aware of that. Robert says, "he thinks he has convinced his friends that he has changed, but again, I needed to go with him the next time he visits his home state." As the conversation continued, it became clear. Robert asked if Oliver needed money for "car trouble." I said yes, which I thought was weird because he had the brakes checked and an oil change; even the neighbor mechanic had looked at his car before he left. Robert asked if I had asked for a receipt, and I said no. Robert told me that the car trouble was most likely because Oliver had given his car to the drug man for drugs.

Some drug addicts obtain drugs by providing the drug dealer their car to pay off their drug debt; once the debt is paid, the vehicle is returned. I was stunned. He said none of Oliver's friends believed any excuses about car trouble and knew Oliver was not communicating the entire truth. The more Robert talked, I knew Oliver was on a drug binged. Many emotions entered my mind; sick, angry, mad, and furious. I thought back to 2018 when Oliver needed $50.00 to get his car back because he had "lost control" and someone had "taken" his car around the corner. Then my mind returned to all the times Oliver had traveled to his home state and disappeared for days without calling me or returning a text.

I told Robert, again, that Oliver had informed me about his past drug problems but had been clean for many years. Robert laughed and explained that when he visited in May 2020, they had visited a friend's father-in-law to buy cocaine. Robert told me that weight loss, dehydration, and irritability are all signs he is recovering from a binge. Robert and I agreed to keep this conversation between the two of us. He said he only gave me this information to help Oliver and to protect me from being taken advantage of in this situation. Robert even informed me that Oliver had stolen money from him years ago. I never told Oliver of the text conversation I had with Robert. However, I kept this information in the back of my mind.

In June 2021, Oliver and I planned a vacation to his home state. I was excited to go on a road trip with Oliver, to visit his family, and to see his home state. I was looking forward to getting to know his daughters and grandchildren better. I had never met his youngest grandson and was anxious to meet him. We left Texas early on June 16th and arrived in Illinois on June 17th. After checking into Airbnb, Oliver's daughter and I went for pedicures. Then we went back to his mother-in-law's home for dinner. His ex-wife, daughter, and grandchildren were all there. We had a great time talking and laughing.

The next day was Friday, June 18th; Oliver and I went shopping in downtown Chicago. We went by the Joffrey Ballet and ate some authentic Chicago foods. The trip was going great. Oliver told me he would catch up with some friends later that evening. Oliver stated every Friday, and there is an event where a band plays music behind the museum. Oliver was going to meet some friends there and return later that evening. After leaving me at the Airbnb, Oliver left around 6 pm. This night was the beginning of a terrible vacation.

Saturday morning, June 19th, Oliver had not returned. I texted and called. He immediately texted me back and said he had drunk too much and stayed the night with a friend. I got up, worked out, showered, and prepared for the day. We had planned to meet with his daughters and grandchildren and go out for pizza to celebrate Father's Day. By noon, Oliver had not returned. I called and texted for over two hours, no response. Around 1 pm, his daughter contacted me and said she had been trying to reach her dad. I explained that he had gone out and stayed at a friend's home the night before. I told her that I had spoken with him that morning, and he knew we were supposed to meet for pizza; however, he had not returned yet.

As the day progressed, neither his daughter nor I heard from him. Later that afternoon, his daughter offered to come and take me out. I had to decline because Oliver had the room key, and I would have no way to lock the room. By this time, I was worried and scared. Another resident at the Airbnb had his baby daughter with him. I could hear the resident arguing with his daughter's mother on the phone. They were cursing, yelling, and screaming at one another. I stayed in the room, pacing and worrying; my mind then returned to the text conversation I had with Robert in March. Now I understood when he said I should go with him when he went to Illinois. I started wondering how my presence could make any difference. Oliver was not answering calls, and I had no clue about his whereabouts.

Around 3 pm on June 20th, Oliver called, asking for $130.00. I was furious and immediately began yelling at him. I told him we missed dinner with his family. I immediately asked him about his drug addiction. Oliver's excuse was that he was gambling and lost money. Oliver wanted additional money to attempt to win his money back to pay his debt back. I asked if he was being held against his will. He said no. I told him I was hungry and scared at how the other Airbnb resident acted. He said once he had the money, he could leave. I sent him $130.00. I received verification that he had received the money; however, Oliver never returned. I called, but no answer. Sunday evening, I began looking for a flight home. I was angry, tired, hungry, and furious. I was planning to get an Uber to the airport and fly back to Texas.

Monday, June 21st, desperate, upset, and worried sick about Oliver, I reached out to his best friend, Sebastian, who lives in Texas. I told him the entire story. Sebastian stated that he had not been in contact with Oliver; Oliver was probably on a binger. Sebastian noted that he would make some calls and get back to me. In the meantime, Sebastian asked if I needed anything to let him know. A bit later, Oliver's brother James called me. James stated that he had not heard from Oliver or seen him. James had tried to contact Oliver but did not get an answer. Finally, Oliver returned around 4 pm after being gone since Friday evening. He was dirty and smelly. I yelled, screamed, and told him how angry and disrespected I felt. He admitted to drinking and doing drugs. He said he "went around the wrong crowd" and thought he had the power to resist. Oliver showered and said he would take me to get something to eat after going to help a friend of his. After helping his friend, we had dinner and returned to Airbnb. The following day, at the advice of Oliver's friend, I tried desperately to talk Oliver into returning to Houston immediately. Oliver's friend felt that Oliver being in Chicago would only increase his craving for drugs. He even suggested I leave him there and drive back alone if Oliver refused to leave.

The original plan was to fly back to Houston on June 23rd, as I had to return to work on June 24th. Oliver was to remain in Illinois; I flew back to Illinois on Thursday, July 1st. We were scheduled to attend a party on July 3rd, go for a barbeque on July 4th, then do more touristy stuff on July 5th. Then, on July 6th, we would visit his family that morning and leave for Texas. Oliver was resistant to the idea but then agreed and changed his mind. I also told him we both needed some drug treatment counseling sessions immediately. Oliver needed help, and I needed to understand addictions. He agreed but still refused to drive back to Texas. We got up and rushed to pack on June 22nd; we needed to be out of the Airbnb by 11 am. Oliver could barely move. I had to drive to the hotel we were staying at for the night because I could not stay awake, as Oliver was coming down from his drug high.

We arrived at our hotel around 1 pm. I wanted Oliver to go shopping, but Oliver could barely move. I went shopping by myself. I was still hoping to convince him to return to Texas, but he refused. The following day, June 23rd, I flew back to Texas. I was super worried about Oliver, who seemed normal when I departed. He promised me he would go to Indiana and avoid drugs. Later, I found out that it never happened.

I returned home on June 23rd. Oliver called me and said he was visiting some friends. His childhood friend, who he grew up with, was in Chicago. They were at his sister's home and planning to have a birthday celebration for him. Oliver asked me to send him $100.00, so he could help buy food, which I did.

The next day, June 24th, Oliver called and asked for $100.00. He said he needed gas money and some money for food. So, I sent him $100.00. He mentioned that he did not go to his brother's Indiana home on June 23rd because he was celebrating his friend's birthday late. He said he was going to his brother's house that day. We talked briefly on Friday, June 25th, but not on June 26th. On June 27th, I called Oliver. He said he was grateful I called because his phone was disconnected. Oliver's following statement was that the bank had contacted him about fraudulent activity on his debit card and shut it down. Since his bank is only located in Texas, a new debit card was issued, but the bank would only send it to Texas.

Therefore, Oliver had no access to his money, and he stayed with his friend Mark and his wife, Vanessa. They were an older couple, and Mark used a wheelchair. Oliver said he helped them out and was happy to spend time with Mark. Due to the issue with the debit card, he had been unable to pay for the Airbnb we were booked to stay at when I returned on July 1st. I told him to pay for it with my debit card. He also asked for $40.00, which I did send him. I did not hear from Oliver on June 28th or June 29th. I started to feel apprehensive about going back on July 1st. I did talk with Oliver on June 30th; he said the Airbnb that we stayed at previously was no longer available. He said the internet connection at home was not good but that he would find another Airbnb. As I was sitting at the airport, we talked again on the morning of July 1st. My first action was to pay Oliver's phone bill so we could talk without me having to call Mark's home. Oliver booked the Airbnb, and everything seemed settled for part two of the trip.

I arrived in Chicago late July 1st. Oliver looked good, healthy, and happy. We checked into the Airbnb and had dinner. That Friday, July 2nd, we went to the beach and had a relaxing day. Saturday, July 3rd, we went to a friend's party. We returned late that night. Oliver dropped me off and said he would look for a parking spot. He did not return for over 45 minutes; panic struck. Oliver would not answer his phone; finally, after an hour, he said that the police saw him driving around and had stopped him. Unfortunately, I had his wallet because he had no pockets. I was up all night, communicating sporadically with Oliver. He said the police were stalling to release him. However, when they let him go, which Oliver said was around 7 am, the morning of July 4th, he said he went to his old neighborhood to borrow gas from a friend. He said he was waiting for his friend to return with the money. I asked him why he did not ask me for help. Oliver said I had his identification, so he could not pick up money if I sent it to him. Finally, around 11 am, Oliver returned. He did not seem high or under the influence; however, he was tired and angry. To this day, I never questioned the truth of this story.

On the morning of July 5th, we did some sightseeing and hung out, and had a great time. We went to his ex-mother-in-law's home to say goodbye to his children and grandchildren. Also, he wanted his brother-in-law to look at his car because the check engine light was on. Oliver disappeared for over two hours and would not answer the phone. I sat embarrassed in front of his ex-mother-in-law home. Finally, around 10 pm, he returned to pick me up. He was high on marijuana. Then he informed me that he would take me back to the Airbnb and then go by a friend's home to take him somewhere.

I had had enough of the stories and excuses; I was on vacation. Instead, I sat in the room; I was going along. Oliver said he did not want me in that part of town. I told him he shouldn't be there if it was the wrong area. Oliver did just what he wanted to do.

He picked up his friend and then took me to the Airbnb. I pleaded with him not to leave; he looked at me coldly and said, "I will be right back." I sarcastically said, "yeah, see you in a few days," and slammed the door in his face. Oliver returned at 5 am. I am furious because we had to check out by 11 am and drive home. Plus, due to his money problems, I was draining my bank accounts, ensuring we had enough to get home. I yelled at him and told him once again he showed me no respect and did "just what he wanted to do." I told him the entire trip was a nightmare, and I wanted to go home. During the vacation, we never saw his brother or mother nor spent more than a few hours with his children and grandchildren.

We left on the morning of July 6th. I had to drive because Oliver was still high and sleepy. We had to stop to pick up his computer, which he said had a broken screen. The computer repair place was also a pawn shop. I believe now that he had pawned the laptop for $200.00. He had told me not to worry about paying for it, but I knew he needed the computer for school. I let him have it about his behavior and how I wanted a vacation to relax after a long, challenging school year. Instead, vacation was a nightmare. We stayed outside Chicago on July 6th and returned home on July 7th. I got back to work, and the new school year began. I never followed through with getting drug counseling for Oliver or me. Life returned to normal. Oliver returned to work and continued school to work on his degree. His various friends talked to him about his behavior during our trip.

November 2021, during a 4-day weekend. I visited my brother in Michigan while Oliver traveled to Chicago. Interestingly enough, before leaving, Oliver received a text from his mother. It was a very mean text. He had informed her that he was going to Chicago in November. She sent a nasty text saying that the only reason he goes to Chicago is to get high and all his ex-wives, brother, and family knew what he was doing. She mentioned that another friend of his did drugs so much that it sent his mother to an early grave. Ironically, this was the friend Oliver would stay with during his trip. I asked him why his mother would say something so mean and what prompted this. Oliver said she was being mean, and what she said about his friend occurred many years prior.

I paid for him a rental car, and he paid me back (before leaving). He flew to Chicago on October 28th and was scheduled to return on November 1st. I left on October 29th to return on November 2nd. On October 31st, Oliver called and asked for $300.00. He said that even though the rental car was paid for, he needed to leave a $300.00 deposit. He said he put the deposit on his credit card and did not have spending money. So, I sent him $300.00 and never heard from him again. I even mentioned to him that he only called me for money, never asking how my trip went or if I needed anything. On November 1st, Oliver never returned home, nor did he call. Maybe he decided to stay another day and waited for him to call. Oliver called late that night, stating that he had missed his flight. Thinking about who he stayed with, his mother's text, and the fact that I had not heard from him, I immediately asked what was happening. I was furious that he had just called me, and Oliver was still in Chicago. He said he was running late and knew he would not have time to return the rental car and make his flight.

On top of that, his phone was off again as he had not paid the bill. Oliver said he would be home tomorrow, November 2nd. He gave me a number where I could reach him. I called him when I arrived at the airport early on November 2nd; I told him to pay his phone bill immediately (I gave him my debit card) and told him I would call when I landed in Houston. I called him when I arrived in Houston, and he said he would be home later that day. Around 1 pm, I received an emergency call from him. He said that the airline treated his missed flight as a no-show and made him pay for a ticket home. I had to pay $250.00 for a ticket home for Oliver and send him $110.00, so he would have cash on hand. I began to wonder if drugs were an issue. I questioned him when he returned; he denied any wrongdoing other than he ran late and missed his flight.

Fast forward to 2022, Oliver's drug use took a wrong turn. On Saturday, March 12, 2022, he went to a friend's home to help with some DJ equipment. He called later and said he was on his way home. But by 9 am, he had not returned. I called him, and he said he had detoured to Sebastian's home to watch his son for a few hours because Sebastian had to take his wife to the hospital. He apologized for not calling and said he was on the way home. By 11 pm, Oliver was not home, so I called. He answered that he was at a neighbor's home; however, I did not see the car. I looked outside and saw his car. He said he was on the run with the neighbor, a tow truck driver. I went to bed. I woke up on Sunday, March 13th, and looked outside. Oliver's car was gone. I figured he went to the store because he was supposed to go the day before. I called him, no answer. I called all morning long, no answer.

I still had not heard anything by noon, and Oliver was not home. I called his friend, Sebastian, to see if he had heard from him. Sebastian informed me that he had seen Oliver the night before; they had a beer and watched some basketball. Sebastian mentioned nothing about Oliver watching his son or wife go to the hospital. I did not mention it either. I explained the situation to Sebastian, and he said by this time, you should know the pattern. He tried to call Oliver but got no answer

At this point, I panicked and thought the worst; Oliver had never disappeared in Houston. I continued calling and texting Oliver that I would call the police unless I heard from him. I called, and no answer. I finally talked to the neighbor, Juan, and his wife, around 4 pm. He said Oliver had spent the night at his home and left around 7:30 am. He saw him get into the car and leave. He said he called and suggested Oliver; go home; however, Oliver told him he was going to the store for me. The neighbor tried calling him, as did his wife, but there was no answer. I called the police. During this time, Oliver's brother called, saying he could not get ahold of him. I told him what was going on. The Sheriff, against my wishes, called his daughters, who then called me to find out what was happening.

Finally, around 10 pm, Oliver called me. When I answered, he was calm and acted like nothing was wrong. He said he was with some friends and asked for $50.00. He said he was gambling with friends and lost some money. I again asked if he was being held against his will, and he said no. I asked him why he could not get the money and then return to pay the person. He replied that he did not want to leave owning a debt. He said, well, the sooner you send the money, the sooner he can leave. I sent him $50.00, but he did not return until 5 am Monday, March 14th. I called his brother and daughter to let them know that Oliver was okay and that I had heard from him.

He slept all day Monday (it was spring break week for us). It was Tuesday when we discussed the incident. Oliver told me not to contact his family and friend. I told him that HIS lack of communication caused me to fear for his safety and call the police. He never apologized for his actions. Months later, I found out from my neighbor, Juan, the tow truck driver, that Oliver had told several lies. Oliver never went on a tow truck run with him. He told me Oliver called him around 6 pm Saturday after helping his friend, asking him to come to a bar. Juan observed Oliver with some friends, paying everyone's bar bill while celebrating passing his mid-terms. He said that Oliver stayed at his home, and they sat in the garage, talking, and Oliver was getting high.

In April 2022, Oliver decided to travel to Illinois for his grandson's birthday. I was a bit fearful because every other Illinois trip had resulted in him not calling me for days, and when he did call, he always needed money. He said he would stay with his daughter, which made me more at ease. Oliver left on April 14th and traveled by plane. I called Oliver on April 15th and said he could not get a rental car because they would not split the deposit between two credit cards. We talked, and he asked if I could loan him $500.00 for the rental car. He said his good friend would give him the money to give back to me, and he would pay him back. It sounded odd, and I asked Oliver why the friend could not just give him the $500.00. He said his friend would not get paid until later and would give him the money on Monday, April 18th, when he drove Oliver to the airport. I gave him the $500.00. He called me on Saturday, furious because he still could not get the rental car. We laughed and said at least he didn't have to pay anyone $500.00. We talked a few times on Saturday, April 16th, and 17th, Easter, and I didn't hear from Oliver until the evening, which made me angry. He said he was stuck at his mother-in- law's home; Oliver had stayed there (and not at his daughter's home because he could not reach his daughter. Oliver complained about being bored but was calling so I could help him complete a school test online. We agreed to Zoom at 6:30 pm.

I called, and Oliver never answered. I was worried because this assignment he had to finish was a test. Oliver never called back. Monday, April 18th, I heard nothing from Oliver all day. His brother called me, asking if he had returned home. He said Oliver never called, texted, or visited him during his time there. I told his brother that I had spoken with him Sunday evening, and his flight was Monday, April 18th, in the evening. I fell asleep early on April 18th and woke up around 10:30 pm in a panic. Oliver had not called and was not home. His flight was due in at 8:30 pm. I called him immediately, and Oliver said he was okay and still in Chicago. Oliver said he was on the phone with the airline, changing his flight.

At this point, I was getting angry because I saw the pattern. On every Chicago trip, Oliver would disappear, and the only communication was for money. Oliver begged me for $100.00, so he could get a hotel. I told him no and to go back to his mother-in- law's home. He said he did not want to go back there so late as it was after 11:00 pm. After arguing back and forth, I gave Oliver $100.00 and hung up on him. He texted and thanked me for the $100.00, said he got a hotel and promised things would be different. Oliver returned home on Tuesday, April 16th, around 10:30 pm.

The following day, I asked for the $500.00 his friend was supposed to give him. He said he didn't have it. I walked out of the house and slammed the door. Later that day, Oliver gave me $600.00 and said he had taken out a title loan. He never admitted to using drugs; he said he went out partying. However, I am confident that he met up with friends late on Sunday, April 17th, and did drugs; this is why he missed his flight, spent my $500.00 on drugs, and ran out of money.

Fast forward to later that month, Saturday, April 30th. I had to work that Saturday. Oliver called and said he was going with his friend, Sebastian, and another person to listen to house music at an event in Houston. I called him when I left work. He asked if I wanted to go the next day because the music there was a music brunch. I said yes. After this conversation, around 1:00 pm, I did not hear anymore from Oliver, and he did not come home. Sunday, May 1st, he called me in the morning. He said he was on the way home. I immediately got angry and told him that, once again, he did not communicate his

54

whereabouts and never came home. He said he stayed at a friend's home. I heard nothing more from Oliver that day.

I went to work on Monday, May 2nd. I watched my house alarm app to see if Oliver had come home. He came home around 11:30 am, then left again around noon. He never called me until around 3:30 am on Tuesday, May 3rd. I did not speak to him. When I arrived home from work, I did not answer the phone at 9 pm (on May 2nd). He returned later that day, heard the shower, and asked, "where I was going which was not an appropriate question coming from him. He offered no information about where he had been. I went to work on Wednesday, May 4th, when I obtained an alert that Oliver set the house alarm around 11 am. He did not return. Thursday, May 5th, Oliver texted me around 10 am. He said he had checked himself into rehab, and they had kept him overnight for detox. He said he was coming home today and would attend Thursday's meetings.

Later, I found out this was also a lie. Sometimes, during this week, his brother called me and asked if Oliver was okay. He said Oliver had called him on Monday, May 2nd, and said he was partying and had asked to borrow money. I told him that Oliver had "disappeared" again. I was more concerned that he did not go to work the entire 1st week of May. Of course, I was asked by him to help forge a doctor's note, excusing him from work. He also asked me to loan him money to pay his ex-wife and brother back, as he had borrowed money from them earlier that week.

In June 2022, Oliver and I were supposed to attend a friend's birthday party on Saturday, June 11th. This friend helped back in March. Before the party, we were informed that not many women would be there, and I should stay home; Oliver went. He kept reassuring me he would be back that night. He drove my car because his car inspection had expired, and he didn't want to be stopped possibly by the police, especially since he would be returning late. I gave him my debit card to buy dinner and gas in my car. Oliver called me at about 2:45 am on Sunday, June 12th. He said they had just "shut the party down," and he would stay at his friend's home. I thanked him for calling and went to bed. 7 am Sunday, Oliver called and said he could not find the car keys. He said he had looked everywhere and could not find them. I told him I had a spare set and would bring them to him. He insisted on me not coming and said he would get our neighbor, Juan, the tow truck driver, to get him. I told Oliver I would bring him the keys. Again, he kept saying he was trying to do the right thing and didn't want to put me out. I saw him pull into the gas station, which was the last time I would see him for two days.

I arrived back home around 8:30 am. I thought, here we go again. However, I stayed calm and asked Oliver to let me know he was okay. I texted and left several voice messages; I used a calm voice in all my messages. That same day, my mom went to the hospital. I even told Oliver this via text message and asked him to let me know that he was okay as I was now worried about my mom and him. Oliver never called nor came home. He did send a message around 9:30 pm, saying he was on his way home. He still had my car and debit card. My gut told me to lock my credit card, but I did not listen to my heart. I woke up in a panic around 3:30 am and checked my bank account. $100.00 was missing from my savings. I locked my card and sent Oliver a message, telling him he had crossed the line stealing money from me and that my card was now locked.

Monday, June 13, was my 1st day of work for summer school. I was stressed and angry. On the way to work, Oliver called twice, but I did not answer. I was even more furious because he had my car with my work identification. Around 5 pm, Oliver sent a text begging me to answer the phone. He said he was in rehab and could not have his cell phone during detox; however, since he was on a break, he was trying to call me. His discharge counselor said Oliver was ready to return home and needed gas money. I told Oliver he could come home, but I was not prepared to talk. I asked why do you need $20.00 when Oliver had stolen $100.00 from my savings. Oliver claimed he had to stay at a halfway house before going to rehab. I did not believe his story.

I only sent him money because I needed my car, debit card, and work ID back. Then Oliver said he would stay there to watch a little of the basketball game and then come home. I found this statement odd because if you are discharged from a hospital, you don't just hang out and leave when you want. Oliver assured me he would call when he left. At 11 pm. Oliver had not called. I called him; he said he was on the road but was too tired to drive. He said he didn't want to have an accident so that he would stay the night at the rehab facility. I told him I had to leave for work no later than 6 am and I needed my car. He assured me he would be home in time.

Tuesday, June 14th, I called Oliver, no answer. I waited until 6 am and then left for work. Oliver called around 6:10 am and said he was on his way home. I told him I had to go because I had to be at work by 6:30 am. He said he thought it was 7 am. He said he would bring my identification to the school; I hung up on him. He never returned my car or identification to the school. He refused to answer any calls and text messages that day, despite me saying I could be sent home and lose a day's pay for not having identification two days in a row. I heard nothing from Oliver; he arrived home around 10 pm that night. He returned my card and my keys but said nothing. I immediately hid my keys and debit card in my pillowcase. I went to work on Wednesday, June 15th. It was dark when I left the house and when I arrived at work. When I went to my car, at the end of the day, I got a big shock. Oliver had been in an accident with my vehicle. The entire driver's side was damaged with black marks and scars. I was furious and screamed most of the drive home. I went home and said nothing to Oliver, who was asleep. We did not speak that evening. I was looking for drug treatment because I knew he had gotten paid on June 14th. I thought this would be the perfect time to get him some help if he was out of money.

Thursday, June 16th, Oliver took off again. I was at work, but I was monitoring the house alarm app. He left around 2 pm, returned around 3 pm then left again. When I got home from work, I noticed that he had taken one of his expensive DJ equipment. He returned around 1:30 am Friday, June 17. Oliver went into the bedroom drawer and explained he would return. I immediately searched the garage but found nothing. He began calling me the morning of June 17th around 7:30 am. I refused to answer. He came home around 9 am, fussed at me for not answering the phone, gave me back the $100 he had stolen from my account on June 12th, then left again. I searched the drawer where he took the money; I found a receipt where he had pawned his DJ equipment for $700.

At this time, I knew the addiction was terrible. He returned sometime Sunday, June 19th. He slept for two days. I did not speak to him for several days. Oliver did not shower for several days; he barely ate but drank lots of water. His daughter and brother called me, asking if he was okay. I did tell them what was going on and that I was trying to find treatment for Oliver. Later, I found out that he had borrowed $100 from his daughter and money from his brother.

Oliver stayed home the week of June 20th because he was out

of money. I reached out to his friend, Sebastian, on June 20th for advice. I told him what had been happening and that Oliver had pawned his DJ equipment. I explained to Sebastian that I had put the pieces together. I noticed that every time Oliver visits this one friend, he disappears. Sebastian confirmed that this friend has a friend with a drug hook-up. Sebastian said he even talked to this person and warned him about Oliver. Sebastian advised me to find a rehab for Oliver or leave him until he got help. I worked all week on finding treatment for Oliver.

I went to parking lots after work to make calls. Sadly, with insurance, Oliver's co-pay would be $3,000. I then looked for free rehab; those facilities were in drug- infested parts of town. On Saturday, June 25th, Oliver got up early, showered, and said he was going to his Narcotics Anonymous meeting. Oliver did not return. I called and texted him, no response. He called me around 6 pm and asked for $25.00. He said he needed $25 to pay a debt to a friend, and then he would be home. I told him I did not believe him. Oliver never came home. He called again, around 10 pm, asking for another $25. Oliver begged me to talk to his friend and swore they were not using drugs, and his friend would prove it. Oliver had left money on the dresser he needed for a car repair. I sent the $25 that was left on the dresser. I heard no more from him; he did not return until Monday, June 27th, while I was at work. He slept for two days. In the meantime, I was desperately trying to find a rehab.

Oliver was gone from June 29th to July 2nd. When he returned on July 2nd, he slept for about three days. We barely spoke. I did threaten to leave him. I told him I was not going to live like this. Oliver said I lacked understanding, and he was going someplace so he would not use drugs. I laughed in his face and called him a liar. I told him I knew he had lied about going to rehab because detox lasts days, not just a few hours. Oliver yelled back, so you know everything about drug treatment? During the next week, he drank a lot of water, watched television all day, and barely showered.

On June 30th, I contacted Oliver's friend, Robert, and his wife, for counsel. Robert's wife has been an enormous help to me. I spoke with Robert on July 1st. Robert said he had reached out to Oliver sometime early that morning. Oliver asked him for $25.00. He said he gave Oliver the money; Oliver told him he had spoken to me and knew what was happening. Oliver said I was trying to make him look bad.

Robert told Oliver to call him when he got home and to put me on the phone so that he would know that Oliver was home.

When Oliver returned on July 2nd, he said nothing of his conversation with Robert. I overheard them talking; he told me that Robert was never allowed in the house again. As soon as Oliver arrived home, Juan immediately demanded his battery back. Oliver was furious and when on and on about how he gave Juan money and never asked for it back, yet Juan took his battery back. Oliver refuses to speak to Juan and gets mad when I talk to him.

Oliver was home for two weeks as he had no car battery. It just so happened I was on vacation the week of July 4th. I returned to work on July 11th. Oliver showed signs of his old self. He talked about starting school in August and looking for a job. Oliver said he found a used battery at the hardware store. But I was fearful because payday was coming; Oliver would get paid on July 14th. He asked me to jump his car the morning of July 14 and said he was going straight to the hardware store, which opened at 8 am. I battery jumped his car, and he left it running in the garage with the garage door half opened. Around 2:30 pm, Oliver called and asked for $100. He said his car was acting up and not accepting a jump. He said he was at Ace Hardware trying to get a battery. I was confused and questioned him because he was supposed to have purchased the battery that morning. He brushed me off and said he was now trying to get the battery. He said he had $400 in the drawer at home, and I could take my $100 out of that money. I sent Oliver the $100 and called him to confirm he received it. When I got home, I took the money from the dresser. I looked at my house alarm app. Oliver had set the house alarm at 6:30 am and had not returned. I called and texted him, but he did not respond. Oliver did not come home that night; he did call me around 11 pm, but I was asleep.

Oliver began calling around 1:30 am the morning of July 15th; he called several times over 45 minutes. I ignored him; I knew all he wanted was money. Around 7:30 am, he called me again; I did not answer. Then his mother called me, but I did not answer. His mother left a voice mail message, stating that Oliver was trying to get ahold of me. She said he was being harassed by the police and needed me to call asap. I was suspicious; however, Oliver does not have a good relationship with his mother, so I thought there might be some truth to the story. So, I gave in and called. Oliver flew into a rage, yelling at me for not answering the phone and needing to borrow money to bond out of jail. I sent him $100.00, but Oliver never came home.

Through all of this, I am struggling with whether to continue the relationship. I know that Oliver needs help. Deep down, he is a good man who loves his friends and family. I even told Oliver was no longer the man I initially loved. There are days that he breaks into tears because, at 58, he is still trying to finish his college degree. He will say that, at 58, he has nothing and has never earned an income over $40,000 yearly. Since moving to Houston, he has worked at three different school districts, where he feels he is being treated unfairly. However, after seeing his behavior over the last few years, I wonder if the school is mistreating him or if his behavior has played a significant part. I don't know. He even said that the constant setbacks in life are part of why he started using drugs again. I've continued to cut him off entirely financially. I won't even give him money for a haircut. I am doing all the work to get him some help.

Ironically, Oliver never offered a solution or any place to seek treatment. This action proves that he never sought drug treatment or went to Narcotics Anonymous meetings. I've given him a list of Narcotics Anonymous meetings that Oliver can attend, at least to get strength and advice from others dealing with the same thing. He does not go. Oliver has access to two free sessions with a counselor through the school district. The school district offers this to all employees, which is strictly confidential. I have encouraged him to use this resource, but he won't.

At times, he is distraught by my actions regarding reaching out to his two closest friends for help and telling his business. He refuses to realize that his actions caused me to seek the help of his friends, to try and talk with him about his behavior. He has accused me of spreading our business to his friends and embarrassing him. I've tried to explain to him that I was worried and scared for him; I was trying my best to get someone he may listen to talk with him. But Oliver has chastised me for my actions.

When I try to tell him my feelings, he shuts me down immediately and claims to know how resentful, used, disrespected, and ignored. He will respond in one way when I express my feelings: he will listen briefly and walk away. Oliver does not understand how failing to tell the truth about going to rehab, his drug use, lack of communication, need for money, and lies about why he needed money, being gone for days, will destroy trust in a relationship.

Since he has been home, I have hidden my purse and car keys every night. I've moved my two credit cards from the fireproof safe to another location. I refuse to allow him to drive my car; I won't even allow him to drive from the driveway to the garage. Oliver needs therapy to deal with his drug issues and the issues that causes him to relapse. Chicago is a big trigger for him. I will try to get him some help while deciding whether to continue this relationship. However, I believe a truck stop ministry would help both of us. I would be able to understand addictions and develop patience dealing with someone on drugs, and it would give Oliver a source to communicate with since we live around the corner from the truck stop.

Comments and Supporting Data for Respondent Three

Respondent three provided a highly detailed letter of the struggles faced in a relationship when one of the partners has an addiction. Although Respondent three wrote a lengthy letter, it was essential to see and feel the pain of addiction. One of the critical factors of this letter is that The Respondent realized that both people in the relationship needed counseling. The addiction had destroyed the trust within the relationship.

This letter dealt with several issues that arise from addiction—mental abuse, lying, enabling addiction, theft, loss of employment, and financial strain. Respondent Three appeared to need immediate counseling to help deal with the situation. Because most therapists require an appointment, the Respondent realized how helpful it would have been to go to the truck stop around the corner to discuss, seek guidance, and receive knowledge of resources available in the community. Respondent Three's comment supported the need for a truck stop ministry. The ministry is beneficial for both the community and truck drivers.

Respondent Three realized that help was needed to assist with the addiction. Both individuals were suffering from not understanding how to overcome the addiction.

"According to Corey, in cognitive therapy, clients learn how to identify their dysfunctional thinking. Once clients identify cognitive distortions, they are taught to examine and weigh the evidence for and against them. This process of critically examining thoughts involves empirically testing the evidence. Cognitive therapy is focused on present problems, regardless of a client's diagnosis. The past may be brought into therapy when the therapist considers it essential to understand how and when certain dysfunctional beliefs originated."[4]

When addressing and working with addiction, it is essential to look at the biblical references associated with the struggle. Respondent Three needed hope. Therefore, having a biblical counselor or guide at the truck stop would provide the individuals with spiritual guidance.

"When a chemical interfaces with a person's productivity, tranquility, efficiency, or well-being, and when a person is made aware that this is happening but still persists in using the chemical, then that person is addicted, at least psychologically. If one gets physically ill when the drug is withdrawn, then there is a physical dependency.

An addiction is any thinking or behavior that is habitual, repetitions, and very difficult or impossible to control regardless of the consequences. Usually, the addiction brings-short term pleasure, but there are long-term consequences in terms of health, relationships, psychological well-being, and spirituality. Spiritual emptiness, broken bodies, destroyed relationships, ruined careers, dulled brains, deep feelings of grief, and persisting guilt are among the costs of addictions."[5]

Oliver was suffering from many of the actions listed above. The cravings prevented him from being able to make sound decisions. According to Collins, addiction is a destructive force; however, assisting a person in dealing with addiction continues to be challenging for the church.

---

[4] Ibid., 285.

[5] Ibid., 699.

The Bible does not specify cocaine addiction; however, the biblical reference encourages a person to be wise about the body and how one lives.

> "Be very careful, then, and how you live not as unwise but as wise, making the most of every opportunity because the days are evil. Therefore, do not be foolish but understand what the Lord's will is. Do not get drunk on wine, which leads to debauchery. Instead, be filled with the Spirit" (Eph. 5:15-18, NIV).

Oliver has allowed the drugs to overtake his life. Having biblical counseling would also provide hope. Although the Bible does not describe his drug of choice, the Bible tells Christians to take care of the body. Ephesians 5:18 reminds a Christian to be filled with the Holy Spirit. Therefore, when the craving begins to attack the body on a lonely night, an addict can call on the spirit to help remove the need for drugs.

Respondent Four

I worked as a truck driver for many years. One of the main issues I faced was dealing with my health. Most trucks are not equipped to cook food; therefore, a driver is forced to eat from restaurants. Although restaurant food may taste good, I soon realized it was unhealthy. Over the five years, I have suffered from several health issues. Over the last few years, I have suffered from diabetes. As a truck driver, this disease has been challenging to manage. As a diabetic, I must eat at a particular time and remember to take my medications on time.

When I was first diagnosed, I was overweight. The doctor explained that it was vital for me to lose weight. The weight loss would assist me in keeping my numbers in line. As I thought about what would help, I realized that having support at the truck stop would benefit other drivers and myself. When the idea presented to me about developing a truck stop ministry, I had to stop and think. The more I thought about a truck stop ministry, I realized having someone to speak with outside my home ministry would help me stay on track. It would be nice to have a ministry that also looked at and provided health guidance while providing biblical reference. Therefore, a truck stop ministry is an essential aspect for drivers.

Comments and data for Respondent Four

Respondent Four health appeared to be essential to gaining a proper perspective of their understanding of obesity. According to Zoe, one of the first actions one must understand is that a change is needed. A person's current diet must change to decrease obesity.[6] Respondent Four learned that a change was needed in his body. Their current diet wasn't providing all the necessary nutrients to prevent the body from becoming obese. "Obesity was traditionally defined as an increase in body weight that was more significant than twenty percent of an individual's ideal weight – the weight associated with the lowest risk of death, as determined by certain factors, such as age, height, and gender."[7]

The action affects other body areas when a person suffers from a nutritional disease. Some individuals begin to suffer from chronic illness, heart disease, stroke, cancer, and diabetes.[8] Respondent Four realized that it was essential to reduce the fat in their body to decrease the amount of sugar intake to the body. However, the one crucial area in Respondent Four's writings is the importance and the need for guidance in understanding healthy nutrients. Therefore, having a truck stop ministry within the truck stop could benefit the drivers by providing advice on healthy eating.

The Bible provides many references related to caring for the body. Proverbs 25:27 reminds humanity to eat in portions and reframe from over-eating. However, 1 Cor. 10:31 is one of the essential Scriptures related to the proper nutrition of the body. This Scripture tells humanity to remember that whatever one eats or drinks do it in the glory of God. A truck stop ministry could help drivers understand that in everything one does, God created the body. Although many people have provided readings on the body, one must remember that God created the body; therefore, biblical references will clarify the

---

[6] Zoe Harcombe, *The Obesity Epidemic, What Caused it? How can er stop it?* (Columbia Publishing, 2010), 2.

[7] Ibid., 5.

[8] Ibid.

body's development and nutritional needs.

Respondent Five

My addictions are to nicotine, marijuana, and people. Yeah, I know, right people, a person can be codependent on others. Codependency is a relationship in which one person needs the other, and it becomes a requirement. This assignment was a little challenging for me but very helpful for me. I had to do some research on addiction. It helped me get a better understanding of my addictions. The study led me to some different factors of addiction, such as finding the root of my addiction.

Childhood trauma/ behavior, genes, anxiety, environments, and influences play a role in addiction. I learned the type of addictions like behavioral, substance, and impulse addictions. I realized addiction was set up for me to have trouble; I had no way of controlling that fact. My life was set up for an addiction pathway. It was hard to identify because I was a young child. Writing a paper about my addictions was a tremendous help to me on the path to recovery and healing.

Trauma plays a significant role in addiction. Trauma is an emotional response to a terrible event. One way to find your addiction is to understand your addiction's root cause. Some roots of addictions are loneliness, fear, shame, grief, anger, and hereditary factors, along with physical, spiritual, sexual, and emotional abuse. Those traumatic factors can grow into addictions, religions, sex, gambling, people, work, food, drug, and alcohol. One can easily access the drug, due to their family environment and drug history influence.

My mother used drugs, even though she was pregnant. So, you see, I was born with drugs in my system. My mother's choice to use drugs tremendously affected my life in various ways. I should have been able to look up to my mother while she trained me to become a lady. She wasn't able to fulfill that role in my life. My dad worked hard and was a great father. My father was family oriented and raised me in the church. His family originates in Alabama. I couldn't see them that often; however, we went on a family trip every summer. He made my life feel somewhat normal. However, his time was short; he was diagnosed with cancer. When I was seven, he passed away.

I was left with my mother to take care of me. That's when I develop more trauma and anxiety. As time went on, my oldest brother turned 18 years old. He decided to take action in trying to change his sister's environment. My brother and his wife became my guardians. This transition was a challenging phase in my life, along with the trauma and anxiety I had built up.

The way I could deal with my feeling was to give my guardians a hard time while raising me. I displayed anger for no reason. I was dealing with grief. I cried a lot of times, sometimes uncontrollably. I needed help but did not know how to obtain assistance. By the time I turned thirteen, I was totally out of control and ended up in drug and sexual encounters. My brother's wife's mother agreed to let me stay with them for a time. I was still angry and disobedient. This move was a highly different form of lifestyle. I lived on a semi. I was home-schooled and helped with keeping the truck clean.

However, I was still rebellious and was eventually sent back to my brother. As I looked back on the situation, this lesson taught me the importance of having my own business and working hard. When this project was explained to me, I immediately wanted to participate as I looked back; truck stop ministry would have been helpful with some of the anger I felt inside. I could have had someone to speak with while away from home.

Comment and Data for Respondent Five

Respondent Five provided a great understanding of dealing with drugs at a young age. Biblical counseling would have been beneficial to this individual. This letter provided an additional part to a truck stop ministry. Many people fail to realize that many drivers have their families with them, and children are at the truck stops. Respondent Five was homeschooled on a semi-truck. Because of limited events for children in the truck stop, the child continued to suffer from anger and self-control. A truck stop ministry would have opened the door for the child to communicate and the development of social skills.

The critical area of this letter is the individual suffering from co-dependency. One must remember that addicts depend on others. Therefore, this child was raised to depend on others and never learned independence. The child needed therapy, and psychotherapy behavior theory could have helped to child understand choices. A child must learn how to socialize with others. Mack offered a great approach to biblical counseling; involvement.[9] As a church, one must be under the guidance of the youth. However, Gal. 5:22-23 provides an understanding of the character traits one must display when working in a ministry. As Christian leaders, it is essential to demonstrate love to all people.

Respondent Six

Obesity is a silent addiction. Food addiction is well-known in the American psyche. And when you talk to most people, they recognize that they have a weight problem; they don't know how it grew out of control. Lots of people can tell you when their addiction began; usually, they were always heavy as a child, or they gained weight from depression. But how did one's weight get so far out of control? One becomes accustomed to the subtle changes in appearance.

When I first recognized that I was gaining weight, I was already fifty pounds heavier. Growing up, there wasn't much discipline in my home; dad worked, and mom wasn't good at cooking and didn't want to try, so we ate a lot of fast food. McDonald's, Popeye's chicken, Taco Bell, and Burger King were everyday food sources. And I had access to a multitude of junk food to keep me satisfied; I didn't know how to eat.

In my freshman year of high school, I weighed 315 pounds. Since I had to walk, I stayed at that weight for two years. But before starting my junior year, I chose to involve myself in athletics all year round. I lost 100 pounds and stayed there until I left high school. Since I no longer participated in athletics. I began to eat uncontrollably, and my body started changing. I never had an understanding of how to eat healthily and maintain my weight. Looking back because I wasn't conscious of my appearance and how my body was feeling allowed my weight to balloon out of control. I chose to become a truck driver, which is not the best field to get into if you are not conscious of weight because the gain was subtle and took an extended period.

I went from 275 pounds after my initial weight gain; according to my doctor's records, I gained 10 pounds a year for fifteen years. Less than a pound a month, I didn't notice the change. It was a

---

[9] Wayne Mack, A Practical Guide for Effective Biblical Counseling (Wapallopen, PA: Shepard Press, 2021), 15.

combination of 14-hour workdays where I mainly sat and drove and did not prepare my food. So not only was I inactive, but I made the most convenient food choices, which meant fast food at truck stops.

So, in 15 years, I gained 150 pounds and went from 275 to 425 pounds. I was left wondering what had happened, but even when I decided to change my lifestyle and lose weight, I realized how difficult it was to get away from the things that had made life easier. The sugary drinks, the carbohydrates, the party food, and restaurants. It had gotten to the point where I was physically uncomfortable, so I decided to change. I'm seeing significant changes in myself by becoming conscious of my health. Learning to say no to the cravings and become disciplined has shown me that my relationship with food is unhealthy. If I could go back and give myself advice, it would be to become obsessed with my health. A health-based ministry in the truck stops would assist the drivers. Now I am gaining an understanding of how to eat healthy even though I am a truck driver. Many foods are filling and healthy at the truck stops. It would be good to have someone to speak with at the truck stops to guide me through this struggle.

Comments and Data For Respondent Six

Respondent Six became concerned about his physical appearance and failed to understand his body's transition. A ministry would have benefitted this driver by providing a biblical reference concerning the body's nutrient needs. 1 Peter 3:3-4 tells Christians that God is not concerned about one's looks, but God is worried about one's heart and obedience to God's Word. If a person is provided with a biblical understanding of how to care for the body properly, one may reframe from indulging in foods and drinks that are not healthy. Respondent Six had to learn that sugars are unhealthy and that he had to omit particular food from the body.

"Childhood obesity has become a significant problem in many countries. Overweight children often face stigma and suffer from emotional, psychological, and social problems. Obesity can negatively impact a child's education and future socioeconomic status. In 2004 an estimated nine million American children over age six, including teenagers, were overweight or obese. By 2015, twenty percent of children aged

6 to 19 were obese in the United States."[10]

A truck stop ministry is vital for teaching parents and youth about caring for the body. This driver gained a perspective on the importance of eating healthily. However, a truck stop ministry would continue to enhance one's knowledge both spiritually and biblically.

Respondent Seven

My first drug experience happened many, many years ago. I want to say it was 1976. I was the youngest member of a teenage organization, participating with older choir members. I was always associated with people at least three to four years older than me. I was allowed to be in places I had no business being. I learned at an early age about drugs beginning with marijuana. When I was twelve, I learned how to roll and smoke marijuana. That was a disaster as the weed all fell out; needless to say, I was relieved of my rolling duties. This early exposure had a long-lasting effect on not only the lowering of inhibitions but the lowering of my goals and moral calculations.

By the time I was a senior in high school, I was smoking weed regularly, and my addiction included drinking beer and various hard liquors. During this period, I began planting cocaine seeds to grow resilient roots, which I still struggle with today forty-three years later. My cocaine addiction has landed me in some dangerous and outrageous places. Of course, the jail institutions began to manifest themselves in my life. Because of my actions, I have been incarcerated in more county jails than I care to count. Honestly, none of the action would have happened if I didn't have my ever-pleasant invisible demon talking me into these situations. Many times, it seems that the drug encourages me to seek other options to continue indulging. Isn't there a writing in David that states something about doing that which you shouldn't? Anyway, drugs have sent me into deadly situations, concern-free, with no other concern than obtaining and using more drugs.

Driving on drugs started with the fantastical lie addicts tell

---

[10] Obesity, Encyclopedia Britannica, https://www.britannica.com/topic/Obesity, 1, 8/25/2022.

themselves; I can drive. I need to do this drug to stay awake; let that be my story. My crack and cocaine use flourished cause I was able to dabble anywhere and had the privacy to purchase drugs and remain hidden from the world (or so I thought). I thought it was a secret, yet it was all in my head. I didn't realize the daunting, rugged look I began to wear. Not eating for days and having a minimal way to hydrate me outside liquor and beer tends to show in many ways, yet unseen to the one wearing the look.

Well, now it's time to graduate to crystal meth. Meth has been known as a drug of choice for truck drivers for many decades. This drug keeps the person awake for days as they drive up and down the highway. I have experienced meth not allowing me to sleep for up to four days while piloting an eighty-thousand-pound vehicle down the highway. Drugs have been ingrained in the industry that additional names to associate with their drug of choice; meth is known as Lucille, and high-speed chicken feed, crack is known as white smoke, pocket rockets, and Scotty beam me up.

A truck stop ministry could be the last life preserver thrown to a drowning lonely soul. Many drivers fester alone in their world, unbeknownst to those near that they might be ready to explode. A truck stop ministry would give me an option versus hanging out in the streets seeking drugs. When I heard about this project, I wanted to participate. Change is hard; I hope my story will help a person to reframe from drugs.

Comments and Supporting Data for Respondent Seven

Respondent Seven appears to be seeking help but doesn't have a resource to rely on. Respondent Seven realizes he has an addiction that stems from drug use at an early age. The other important fact about this letter is that the respondent admits to associating with the wrong people. Therefore, Respondent Seven had developed a dependence on the drug. Drugs change the person's perspective and encourage the person to continue taking part in the substance.

"The major problem that arises from the consumption of psychotropic drugs is dependence, the compulsion to use the drug despite any deterioration in health, work, or social activities. Dependence varies from drug to drug in its extent and addict; it can be physical and psychological or both. Physical dependence becomes apparent only when the drug intake is decreased or stopped, and an involuntary illness called withdrawal syndrome occurs. Drugs known to produce physical dependence are opiates and central nervous system depressants such as barbiturates and alcohol. Psychological dependence is indicated when the user relies on a drug to produce a feeling of well-being. This type of dependence varies widely with both substance and user. In its most intense form, the user becomes obsessed with the drug and focuses virtually on his interest and activity in obtaining and using it."[11]

Respondent Seven is not addicted to one drug but to multiple drugs of choice. Therefore, seek each time to obtain a greater drug sensation.

Respondent Seven letter displays an immediate need for a truck stop ministry. Counseling and support are beneficial to the trucking community. Respondent Seven has an addictive behavior due to the different types of drugs they have become attached to over this period.

Collin's stated personality characteristics also play a role. Addictive behaviors and substance abuse may be more likely to develop in people who are impetuous and inclined to act more on impulse than on reflection. Other traits associated with abuse and alcohol dependence are emotional immaturity, limited ability to tolerate tension or frustration, loss of capacity to endure painful or unpleasant feelings, and excessive dependency. Of course, some of these traits may be the result of the addiction instead of or in addition to the cause.[12]

Therefore, biblical counseling would provide additional options for addicts to seek while at the truck stop.

Summary

As stated in the hypotheses of this dissertation: Evangelism will enhance discipleship within the church if the church displays support to the truck drivers by conveying love and including biblical

---

[11] Physical Dependency, Britannia Encyclopedia, https://www.britannica.com/topic/chemical/dependency, 1, 8/25/2022.

[12] Ibid., 686.

counseling. The process is evangelism. Evangelism requires the church to go out into the community and serve others. However, many churches have focused on certain parts of the community and may have failed to realize other needs essential to the community's spiritual growth.

This dissertation has provided a need for a truck stop ministry. The dissertation revealed knowledge about the trucking community by combining biblical references, counseling techniques, and Respondent references of their personal experience. One cannot obtain a proper perspective of the trucking community's spiritual needs without respondents being open to conveying their stories to others. Most respondents wanted to introduce change between the church and the trucking community.

Mark 16:15 God commands the church to go into the world preaching and teaching the word of God. The dissertation has exposed a need for evangelism. The dissertation has covered several addictions that affect truck drivers and the communities. Some form of addiction tempts everyone. However, overcoming the struggle is essential. First Corinthians 10:13-14 reminds Christians to remain faithful to God. Because when one is grounded in God's word, God will answer one's struggle.

This dissertation aimed to provide the churches with insight into the trucking community and the need for spiritual counseling. Many times the trucking community is known as the forgotten. As the world evolves, communities no longer welcome strangers into their society. However, this ministry is an opportunity for churches to come together and learn how to build a ministry that displays love and support to transit individuals and communities.

All respondents were dealing with behavior changes to effect change with their addictions. According to Corey, the counselee needs to understand their thinking and guide the counselee to change.[13] Cognitive Behavior Therapy techniques would assist a counselee in making the adjustments needed to curb their addiction. Most of the respondents realized that a change was needed. However, all agreed that a truck stop ministry and having guidance while away from home is essential to one's growth. By the end of this chapter, the reader should have of the struggle's addicts are facing as well as the

---

[13] 13 Ibid., 274.

information from the specialist. A truck stop ministry is essential to the community to assist in hope and support of the ministry. This chapter aimed to provided detailed information that help the reader understand addictions.

Chapter Four
Evangelism

This chapter will provide a biblical and secular reference in understanding a Truck Stop Ministry. A truck stop ministry is an outreach ministry that provides spiritual formation and healing to a transit community. Many churches have truck stops in their communities. However, some churches fail to offer truck drivers spiritual services. The Church must open its eyes to the 21st century and consider the community's needs, removing the blinders. Many communities have transit individuals who need spiritual fellowship. Throughout the Bible, God instructed people to go outside the Church's walls and serve others. The Book of James begins with one of the best examples of Christian responsibility. "James, a servant of God and the Lord Jesus Christ, to the twelve tribes which are scattered aboard, greeting" (Jas. 1:1 KJV). As a Christian, one must remember that God has commanded servants to go into the world and complete God's mission.

However, evangelism requires a person to be trained and understand God's mission and expectations within the ministry.

Evangelism training is essential. Each Church has a mission. However, if the congregations are unaware of the task, they do not understand the mission's focus. The mission will not be successful.

Imagine the United States Marine Corps, ordered to go into a country. The mission is to rescue a group of Americans taken hostage. The hostages are secured, and the Marines must clear a tunnel blocked with debris to enter the building. It was essential for the Marines to bring specific equipment and ten people per the intelligence information. During the Marine's briefing, the information released only included the rescue of the hostages. When the Marines deployed, the servicemen and women knew the location of the hostages but were not informed of the direction the group should go. Therefore, some of the people went left, right, and straight. The equipment was not present to assist with clearing the debris. The entire group presents is necessary to remove the debris, and only two made it to the locations. What do you feel about the success of this mission? With the lack of organization and vision, the Marines would fail to meet their objectives.[1]

As a Christian, there must be a sense of urgency to ensure group training remains an essential focus in the ministry.

"Perhaps the greatest single weakness of the contemporary Christian Church is the millions of supposed members are not really involved at all and, what is worse, do not think it strange that they are not. As soon as we recognize Christ's intention to make His Church a militant company, we understand at once that the conventional arrangement cannot suffice. There is no real chance of victory in a campaign if ninety percent of the soldiers are untrained and uninvolved, but that is exactly where we stand now. Many alleged Christians do not now understand that loyalty to Christ means sharing personally in His ministry, going, or staying as the situation requires".[2]

This chapter focuses on mission work, training, and development. The Church is not different from the United States Defense Department when it comes to preparing for a mission. Their goal is to protect the well-being of the United States. A Christian mission is to preserve the souls of individuals and develop new disciples. Christ is the Church's body, and the individual churches assist with expanding the body. However, training is essential. Evangelical training is critical in the world. One must understand how to communicate while on a mission is essential to the development of any ministry.

This book focuses on a trucking ministry. The truck stops have people of many cultures and beliefs. One should not expect to learn effective evangelism overnight. Jesus took three years to train the disciples. However, evangelical training is an ongoing process. The training should not focus on one subject; it must include outreach,

---

[1] Julie Smith, *The Development of a Truck Stop Ministry, A Guide for Churches, Schools, and Students* (Charlotte NC: Charlotte Christian College and Theological Seminary, 2021).

[2] Bill Hull, The Disciple-Making Pastor; Leading Others on the Journey of Faith (Grand Rapids, MI: Baker Books 2007), 24.

communication, hermeneutical, and culture training. This book is not saying that to evangelize; one must have a formal degree or attend seminary school. However, when engaging in biblical counseling, one must be trained and meet the state requirement. Of course, this education provides the necessary training to cover this subject. However, anyone evangelizing must train and understand the visions of Christology and God's commission of humanity.[3]

A gallop poll was taken that provided a quantitated understanding, along with the percentage of people who have been trained to go into the world and evangelize.

"A 1980 Gallup poll indicated that of the 22 million churchgoing evangelicals, only 7 percent had taken any evangelistic training, and only 2 percent had introduced another person to Jesus Christ. How would you like to march into battle with only 7 percent of your troops trained and only 2 percent with combat experience"?[4]

This poll supports the need for training. One cannot send a person into battle without the correct tools added to be successful.

The Church's Body

For a Christian to complete a mission, one must first understand the body of Christ. Many people look at the body as an individual entity.[5] However, although the body is one person in the human sense, spiritually, the body consists of many individuals working together to complete a mission.[6] God created the human body to require food and water to maintain its existence.[7] The human body will not survive without nourishment.[8] The human body is limited in its intake.[9] The human body is fragile and requires guidance.[10]

---

[3] Ibid.

[4] Ibid., 24.

[5] Ibid.

[6] Ibid.

[7] Ibid.

[8] Ibid., 24. (All quotes were from the same page).

[9] Ibid.

[10] Ibid.

Therefore, the human body needs others to assist with its survival.[11]

However, the Body of Christ does not need human food for its survival.[12] The spiritual existence of God runs through the veins of the body.[13] The Body of Christ is open to anyone who seeks to enter.[14] It is not limited.[15] God is loving. God loves His creation to seek and accept God's following.[16]

> "For just as the body is one and has many members, and all the members of the body, though many, are one body, so it is with Christ. For in one Spirit, we were all baptized into one body—Jews or Greeks, slaves or free—and all were made to drink of one Spirit. For the body does not consist of one member but many. If the foot should say, because I am not a hand, I do not belong to the body, that would not make it any less a part of the body. And if the ear should say, Because I am not an eye, I do not belong to the body, that would not make it any less part of the body" (1 Cor. 12:12-31 NIV).

God's body does not focus on one race or culture.[17] The body consists of all cultures.[18] No one's refused.[19] God's grace and mercy save anyone who repents and accepts God in their heart. Salvation is open to everyone.[20]

---

[11] Ibid.

[12] Ibid.

[13] Ibid.

[14] Ibid.

[15] Ibid.

[16] Ibid.

[17] Ibid.

[18] Ibid.

[19] Ibid.

[20] Ibid.

A Church On One Accord

For the ministry to remain on one accord, the leader must look at the many examples Jesus used while training the disciples. Jesus began by gaining the disciple's trust. Matthew 4:17-22, Jesus offered the brothers Simon and Andrew an opportunity to follow He, and he would increase their ability to communicate with a human by making disciples. Jesus taught them how to remain faithful and step out on faith. Jesus developed a relationship with the disciples and communicated the mission's goal. Jesus's processes brought the disciples together on one accord.

The Church must remain on one accord. In the Marines' example, their mission failed because their body failed to stay in one accord. The ability to communicate effectively with others is the success of most tasks. Communication is a learned trait. Some people begin at a young age by perfecting their ability to communicate. However, for the church and church group to achieve God's will, being on one accord is critical. The Biblical form of the phrase one accord points out that individuals work for the same common goal. How does a group of individuals get to a common goal? The group must be trained and instructed on the expectations of the mission. The Church will undergo many struggles.

However, the works should not separate the operation of the Church.

The Biblical reference to the Wall of Jericho provided a great example of a church one accord. The Church faced a struggle; however, Joshua instructed the Church not to say a word. Do not discuss our plans. "Then on the seventh day, they got up at dawn and marched around the city seven times in the same manner; that was the only day they circled the city seven times" (Joshua 6:15 KJV). The Scripture states that the group walked around the city in the same manner. At that point, the Church was on one accord. The group remained in the same direction. But what is unique about this mission? The army was in front, and the glory of God was in the back. God's people were experiencing grace and mercy. God's love surrounded and protected His people from danger.

To complete a mission, the church leaders and members must follow the same mission. The leaders must reframe sending others out on a mission without direct direction. Remember, as Christians, we are present to the servant of the kingdom of God; God must be first in Christians' lives. If Christians serve God first, the Holy Spirit will lead the Church in the correct direction. Therefore, missions are created to enhance and support the needs of others.[21]

Preparation is essential to the development of a ministry.

"And the Lord said unto the servants, Go out into the highways and hedges, and compel them to come in, that my house may be filled." (Luke 14:23 KJV). This Scripture is significant in beginning any outreach ministry. God is speaking to His servants and giving directions to His expectations of Christians. The Lord told His servants to "Go." When looking at the word "go," the word means to depart from one location to another. Sometimes the ministry will remove individuals from their comfort zone and relocate them to an area of need. God expects His servant to go out into the world and encourage others to seek God.

Jesus's ministry on earth exists through His ability to go out and reach people with His message. "Learn from Jesus as he keeps company with people who want something."[22] Jesus began his journey by seeking disciples who could continue spreading God's Word. Jesus chose individuals who were open to the calling. Church leaders must seek the right people to head ministries. However, the church leader must train to ensure the congregation understands the Church's vision. Ministry development is an essential part of the Church. God commissioned the Church.

"And Jesus came and spake unto them, saying, all power is given unto me in heaven and in the earth. Go ye therefore, and teach all nations baptizing them in the name of the Father, and the Son, and the Holy Ghost; Teaching them to observe all things whatsoever I have commanded you: and lo, I am with you always, even unto the end of the world" (Matt. 28:18-20 NIV).

---

[21] Ibid.

[22] Adele Calhoun, Spiritual Disciplines Handbook: Practices That Transform Us (Madison, WI: IVP Books, 2005), 7.

Jesus was the best, most incredible trainer in the world. Jesus spoke the truth and treated all of humanity with love. His actions, even today, have never changed. The Holy Spirit continues to work inside Christians, training and developing spiritual growth. The same is needed for those who participate in the truck stop ministry. One must understand and provide necessary services for the community.

Once again, The Book of Matthew recorded that Jesus told His disciples to "Go." Matthew 22:9 also reminded the disciples that their mission is to go out into the community seeking discipleship. The disciples needed to follow the lead of Jesus. Jesus did not just push the disciples out; Jesus provided on-the-job training. Jesus ministered to others while His disciples watched and learned how to communicate with the community. Jesus knew the extent of His Ministry was short. Therefore, Jesus encourages the disciples. Jesus spoke at many gatherings while the disciples observed His knowledge and techniques.

"But Jesus withdrew himself with his disciples to the sea, and a great multitude from Galilee followed him, and from Judaea, and from Jerusalem, and from Idumeans, and from beyond Jordan; and they about Tyra and Sidon, a great multitude, when they heard what great things he did, came unto him" (Mark 3:7- 8, KJV).

Jesus's message resonated with the crowds. The crowds sought to obtain a divine word of hope from Jesus. As Jesus traveled, this Scripture provides insight that the disciples traveled with Him. The disciples gained knowledge of the ministry. During ancient times, the disciples learned that sitting still does not grow the Church. Mark 3:7-8 provides an example of what we call mission today and evangelizing in the world.

In the Scriptures above in the New Testament, Jesus told the disciples to "Go." There should never be a misunderstanding of Jesus's intentions for Biblical leaders. As he began His ministry outside the Church's four walls, the world utilized the identical approach. No longer is the word only available inside the Church. Many are seeking spiritual formation outside the Church. The Body of Christ is expanding. As the Church grows, God's message continues in the 21st century.

The same must happen in a truck stop ministry. Training is essential in the program. A Pastor is not trained in all aspects of counseling.

Therefore, it is essential to develop relationships with others to enhance the ministry.

"But too often, church leader's care for addicts ends with the referral slip. Sometimes the referral can serve as a convenient way to hand off pastoral problems to the real pro. Busy pastors already have a multitude of other pressing concerns on their plates, and pastoral dealings with addicts can be messy and inconvenient. Beyond this, a church leader often feels less equipped than a trained clinician to deal with all the issues that might arise, so there is a certain level of comfort in knowing that the matter is now in the hands of a specialist. This feeling is not just understandable but even commendable to a degree. Pastors should not have to be, or expected to be, the experts in every issue that walks through their door, addiction included. Connection with trusted Christian recovery programs in your area. AA groups and therapists are essential, and you may find some in one's own congregation."[23]

However, training and development are a must need for the ministry. God called Paul. He was not one of the original twelve disciples; God called Paul through the message. Paul did not have the privilege of on-the-job training. Paul learned from the actions and biblical references left by others. Paul's calling is an example of how God can call people in the 21st century. Paul was on a journey to Damascus. Paul did not believe in God and fought against God's word. During Paul's trip to Damascus, God met Him and blinded him. Sometimes, to know God and be known by God, God causes a moment of stillness in one's life, forcing a person to listen to God's message.

"And Ananias went his way and entered into the house; and putting his hands on him said, Brother Saul, the Lord, even Jesus, that appeared unto thee in the way as thou camest, hath sent me, that thou mightiest receive thy sight, and be filled with the Holy Ghost" (Acts 9:17 KJV).

---

[23] Jonathan Benz and Kristian Ross-Dover, *The Recovery-Minded Church Loving and Ministering to People with Addictions* (Downers Grove, IL: IVP Books, 2016), 22.

Paul's focused on the growth of the ministry. Paul had a vision given to him through developing a personal relationship with God. Paul focused on the expansion of the Church. Even as Paul faced persecution, Paul remained focused on the Church. Paul knows he must continue to train and develop leaders for the churches.

Biblical Theology

Paul understood Biblical theology. Paul had faith and believed in Jesus's method.

Jesus's methods encouraged the disciples to display love for all of humanity. Paul sent many letters to the churches, reminding the churches of the love of God. According to LeRoy Aden, "Paul never let us forget that God accepts us despite our being unacceptable, that he loves and forgives even though we continue to show hostility and disbelief toward him. Out of this unconditional, undeserved acceptance flows a love that seeks to serve even as it has been served".[24]

Biblical theology focuses on the study of the whole Bible. Many individuals concentrate on Scriptures that are important to their beliefs. However, the message cannot be conveyed unless Christians focus on the entire Bible. Biblical theology views the importance of one's ability to translate and interpret the Bible. Paul used this in his ministry. Therefore, the truth of Christology remained Paul's ultimate vision.

Anyone planning to develop a ministry must understand Biblical theology, and it is the driving force of the Church. The truck stop ministry is a teaching ministry. The leader must be able to read the ancient text and communicate it to the current day.

However, the leader does not have an in-person relationship with God like the disciples, and all leaders must have a spiritual connection. Prayer and meditation are essential to gaining wisdom and interpreting the biblical Scriptures. Because of Paul's spiritual faith, Paul understood the vision. Paul knew the importance of developing disciples to enhance the kingdom's growth.

---

[24] LeRoy Aden, Pastoral Care, and the Gospel in the Church and Pastoral Care (Grand Rapids: Baker, 1988), 34.

Paul's Vision

Paul displayed some of the most significant examples of a disciple of Jesus. Paul had faith and obedience instilled in his spiritual journey. Paul had a mission to expand the body of Christ. Therefore, he maintained the purpose and vision God had given him. "Nevertheless, he offers a coherent and unwavering view of his purpose as a minister."[25] Jesus displayed a love for all humanity; therefore, Paul showed the same characteristics and passion for the ministry. "He presents a vision of what he wants his communities to become."[26] Therefore, the leader must remain focused like Paul, not wavering and working to better the kingdom.[27]

Paul displayed a love for the community. Even during Paul's imprisonment, his focus was on the Church. Although phones were unavailable for communication, Paul wrote letters to the churches. Paul did not allow his struggle to affect the Church's growth. As leaders, there must be a vision of the ministry. The leader must remain focused on the training and development of the community. The community is a part of the universal body of Christ. The leader may face many struggles and disappointments, even persecution; however, soul-winning and God's kingdom's growth must remain a leader's primary focus.

What Is Evangelism

Evangelism is the preaching and teaching of the Gospel to the world. Many times, the focus is on the four walls of the Church. The four walls of the Church can hinder one's ability to evangelize. One must learn how to communicate and develop effective approaches when ministering outside the Church. The responsibilities and duties, in many cases, keep individuals from learning the real art of

---

[25] 25 James W. Thompson, Pastoral Ministry According to Paul; A Biblical Vision (Grand Rapids, MI: Baker Academics, 2006), 29.

[26] Ibid., 34.

[27] Julie Smith, Paul's Ministry Review (Charlotte, NC: Charlotte: Charlotte Christian College and Theologian Seminary, 2021), PS701 Biblical Theology of Ministry, 2.

evangelism. Evangelism is not an action that comes naturally to some people. Therefore, training is needed to enhance the skills of some individuals.

Sometimes in a small church, members must operate in multiple positions in the Church. The Church had a limited number of members. Instead of focusing on spiritual formation, the focus may become the back functions of the Church, which consist of accounting, paperwork, and other necessary action to enhance the Church. This book is not implying the back function of the Church is not essential. However, the member's spiritual needs must be met.

For example, if a leader fails to evaluate the process, the Church will focus on rituals versus soul-winning. The member held several positions due to the Church's size, which was becoming an overwhelming experience. Therefore, the preparation was intense. Instead of having the opportunity and time to evangelize, the focus remained on preparing for the many programs. Rituals were beginning to develop versus ministering outside the Church to others. However, God instructed the Church to go out and encourage others to accept Christ. All churches must have a form of outreach. Outreach ministry does not mean that evangelism happens only overseas. Communities surrounding the local churches need the support of the local Church. The truck stops are in many communities; however, the Church is not always present. The Church is one body. Therefore, other churches must serve the Church's bodies when individuals are not present in their home church.

As leaders, church responsibilities must not become rituals for the members.

Members need to have spiritual gratification. As the years continued, the programs and activity functions became extreme. Some of the leaders began to step down because of the demand. On this day, after completing all the tasks before the service started and finding a seat, the Pastor stated he was doing something different this week; He planned to choose someone in the congregation to speak. The member sat there and looked around; a feeling came over the member, knowing they would be selected.

The Pastor invited the member to the pulpit. The Pastor had always trained the member to be prepared, and the walk to the pulpit was long. However, their calling was understood. On this Sunday, she preached about David. Although David sinned, he knew God and had a relationship with God. David never stopped and continued to seek God's guidance. A few years later, the member began traveling the United States. While traveling, the member started to meet new people. The interaction with other people opened the door to evangelizing. Although the Church had provided a spiritual foundation at the end of the story, evangelism is essential to any church's and member's spiritual growth.

The four walls of the Church can become a haven and hinder an individual's ability to communicate effectively. Jesus went from location to location, preaching the Gospel. As Christians, God's appointed those to teach and preach the Word of God. Some people are called overseers of the Church, while others evangelize to others outside the Church. However, individuals must remain focused on the purpose and vision of God.

Therefore, it is essential to understand the approaches and worldview.

Deontological

The term deontological means understanding the difference between duty and moral actions. Deontological (απovτoλoγικὴ) is Greek for duty.[28] Therefore, Christians have always to do what is right in the eyes of the Lord. God is the best example of moral character. Therefore, God displays good character. According to Grudem, when his Word declares that he is good, it implies that he considers his own character worthy of approval."[29] God continues to convey His love for humanity, regardless of humanity's sinful nature. God has mercy on and for His creation. When looking at the mercy God displays, one can see that God reveals the Fruits of the Spirit. "But the fruit of the Spirit is love, joy, peace, longsuffering, gentleness, goodness, faith, meekness, temperance: against such there is no law" (Gal. 5:22-23

---

[28] Deontological Ethical, Britannica Encyclopedia, https://www.britannica.com/topic/deontological/ethics, 1, 8/30/2022.

[29] Wayne Grudem, Christian Ethics: An Introduction to Biblical Reasoning (Wheaton, IL: Crossway, 2018), 70.

KJV). God expects His creation to embrace these characteristics. This Scripture proves God's directions and expectations of the moral character of His people.

Deontology is the best example of the actions one should display when dealing with others on ethical issues. A great example of deontological is lying. While ministering at a truck stop, a driver comes to the location needing assistance. As the conversation continues, you discover that the driver lied to their wife. The driver feels terrible about the lie; however, the driver continues to tell different lies to cover up for the first one. He needed to speak with someone for guidance on how to handle the situation. How would one advise the driver?

The deontological ethical view is there is no reason to lie. Therefore, the driver must be honest with his wife about the situation. God provided commandments for the Word. The Old Testament teaches, "Ye shall not steal, neither deal falsely, neither lie one to another" (Lev. 19:11 KJV). A lie must never happen, even if it includes saving the life of another. God expects Christians to have faith in Him. As a human, there will never be an understanding of the will of God. Therefore, Christian faithfulness allows the will of God to take place. God does not need help, nor is there no purpose for any Christian to attempt to change God's character.

God cannot dispute against himself. God will not change His laws or commandments. "Because of the moral standards that God gives us, grounded in his moral character, he could not have made other moral standards for us than the ones that he made. He could not have commanded us that it was right to hate people rather than to love them, lie rather than tell the truth, to murder rather than to protect life, to be unjust rather than just, and so forth."[30]

Utilitarianism

Utilitarianism looks at the moral and ethical decisions of a person.[31] The difference between deontological and utilitarianism, deontological believe there is no excuse for lying, while utilitarianism believes it is essential to look at society's well- being. Will the issue help

---

[30] Ibid., 72-73.

[31] Utilitarianism, Britannica Encyclopedia, https://www.britannica.com/topic/utilitarianism, 1 8/30/22.

the good of most of the people in society? However, this action is not the action of God's will. There are no fallacies in the Word of God. God's Word was given and not changed by the world's values. When dealing with ethical issues, Christians must remember God's importance as one seeks to help others.

When using the same example of the driver lying to his wife, he conveys that he had committed adultery as the driver continues to explain the reason for his lie. After failing to arrive home on time, he discovered that the lady had become pregnant. The driver was distraught because he had failed in his marriage and sinned against God.

Although he wanted to explain everything to his wife, he felt she would seek a divorce. The driver did not want a divorce. Utilitarianism would look at the good of society.

Therefore, to prevent a divorce, the driver could keep the situation separate from his marriage. However, those actions are not the will of God. One must look at the ethical and moral consequences of one's actions.

Ethics

Ethical training is an essential aspect needed when developing a program. Ethical knowledge is vital to anyone who is attempting to communicate with others. Leaders should remember that many people seek reasons to enter legal action. Therefore, this section will assist in providing knowledge of ethical issues that could arise. By the end of this section, the reader will define ethics, understand ethical theories and terminology, and understand potential legal issues.

Some ethical issues a leader faces in a truck stop ministry require professional training. Drug and alcohol abuse is present in the community. Many businesses that sell these items position themselves near a truck stop. This action encourages those who struggle with addiction, providing them with easy access to the articles. Sexual misconduct is another issue within the community. A leader will find many who struggle with the truth of Christianity.

Code of Ethics

The Code of Ethics ensures professionals professionally

conduct their business while providing general guidance when dealing with ethical dilemmas. Before anyone begins to work in the field, there must be an understanding of the ethical practice's expectations. According to Corey and Callanan, "pleading ignorance of the specifics of the ethics code of one's profession is not an excuse when engaging in unethical behavior."[32] The code of ethics looks at several issues; upholding the client's well-being, ensuring a person is working within their competence level, operating ethically and responsibly, and their actions are not harming another.

J. M. Bersoff is a psychologist who believes in the importance of the code of ethics. Bersoff felt there must be a measure created to ensure the safety of others.

> "Realistically, however, what a code of ethics does invalidate the most recent views of a majority of professionals empowered by their colleagues to make decisions about ethical issues. Thus, a code of ethics is, inevitably, anachronistic, conservative, ethnocentric, and the product of political compromise. But recognition of that reality should not inhabit the creation of a document that fully realizes and expresses fundamental moral principles".[33]

Christian leaders are considered professionals. Therefore, it is essential to ensure that Christian leaders are professional and utilize biblical conduct. God was loved and showed love to all who would listen. Therefore, as Christians, one should strive to display the same characteristics.

Ethical Law

Legal issues may arise when working with others in the communities. As a representative of any organization, the individual is

---

[32] Gerald Corey and Marianne Schneider Corey and Patrick Callanan., Issues and Ethics in the Helping Professions (Belmont, OH: Brooks/Cole, 2011), 6.

[33] J. M. Bersoff, Ethical Conflict in Psychology (Washington, DC: American Psychology Association 2003), 15.

considered a professional. Therefore, the individual and organization will be held responsible for unethical behavior.

Discrimination and sexual harassment are a few issues that could arise in the community; when representing the truck stop ministry, it is essential to understand that the representative will face many nationalities and genders. Therefore, the ministry has no room for discrimination of any kind.

The 5 Ethical Characteristics

As leaders, five characteristics must remain instilled in one's behavior while ministering in the community: integrity, impartiality, professional proficiency, confidentiality, and professional conduct. Anyone working with the public in a professional compacity remains subjected to ethical laws. When a person deviates from the rules and procedures of the organization, legal issues can arise. Ethical and moral training is essential to your program's development and should be one of the first training conducted. Let us look at the five ethical characteristics.

Integrity is the ability of a person to stand on moral and ethical principles. According to Trull, most ministers want to be persons of integrity, persons whose professional lives uphold the highest ethical ideals."[34] When a person is leading any ministry, the Word of God is love. Jesus followed the will and directions of God and did not deviate from God's law. Therefore, as God's representative, Christian behavior must exemplify Jesus.

Impartiality is the ability to treat others equally. Equality is an essential aspect of the development of a program. Remaining impartial allows a group to reframe from omitting others from the ministry. The ministry is open to everyone. Social justice has plagued the Western World for centuries. "I had continued to struggle with the central issue, which was the apparent inability, the demonstrable failure of Christianity to deal with a system of social and economic injustice."[35]

---

[34] Joe Trull and James Carter, Ministerial Ethics; Moral Formation for Church Leaders (Grand Rapids, MI: Baker Academic 2004), 15.

[35] Howard Thurman, With Head and Heart (New York, NY: Harcourt Brace & Company 1979), 218.

Therefore, anyone working in the ministry must be open and refrain from discouraging anyone seeking the ministry.

Professional proficiency is having knowledge of a specific profession. As a leader, one must have professional knowledge of the area of scope. Never venture outside one's area of scope. A professional must realize their experience is needed to assist others in dealing with issues. The ministry's goal is not to solve everyone's problems but to provide guidance to allow a person to live in society. Therefore, when creating a ministry, the expertise level of the group must be well-rounded.

Confidentiality is the ability to reframe from divulging other personal information communicated in confidence. Most assume the law profession is the only area that keeps others' information confidential. However, as a minister, others will confide in you and seek guidance. Therefore, a minister must respect those who seek their advice. While working in a truck stop ministry, the leaders will face complex issues without home comforts. Their information must remain confidential.

Profession conduct is professionally always conducting oneself. Professional conduct can become an ethical issue in any organization. As discussed previously, the ministry needs to become well-rounded. One example is adultery. There are many cases of adultery recorded in history. Therefore, a leader must have specific policies and procedures to prevent unprofessional conduct. Women's ministries are needed. The truck stops are filled with both men and women. Sometimes women have actions that require a woman's guidance. "God gifts and calls women and men equally. God intends the male- female relationship to be mutual and in the Church. Her work combined considerable exegetical skill with extensive knowledge of cultural backgrounds".[36]

Ethics

According to Geisler, "ethics deals with what is right and

---

[36] Linda L. Belleville, Women Leaders and the Church Three Crucial Question (Grand Rapids, MI: Baker, 2000), 218.

wrong morally."[37] Geisler provided the best definition of ethics. The trait begins when a child is born. The child starts to learn right from wrong. As the child grows, the learning experiences become a part of the child's character leading into adulthood. Therefore, an understanding of right and wrong remain instilled in the adult. However, the adult must choose what is right and what is wrong.

Moral Ethics is also the principle of determining right and wrong while including socially acceptable in society. Society has set standards on what is permissible in the community. Therefore, in many cases, the concepts clash with biblical references.

Christian Ethics focuses on what is right or wrong in God's view. God has left many examples of proper conduct and His expectations of human life on earth. Therefore, gaining a perspective of God's ethical direction is essential as Christians. Two terms related to this ethical perspective are deontological and utilitarianism.

Professional Behavior

Professional behavior is critical when dealing with others. However, the leader will develop a relationship with the individuals. The connection is essential to the development of the ministry. These men and women are watching the church representative gain ideas about conducting their life as Christians. Ethical behavior helps to provide the encouragement needed to assist the person. Imagine helping a person through a difficult situation while at a truck stop. Instead of remaining professional, the Church's married representative develops a relationship with the individual. "The wisdom literature celebrates the beauty of sex in marriage while at the same time praising faithfulness to one's marriage partner."[38] At that point, the church leader can no longer effectively minister to the community.

Geisler stated that many clergy catastrophes involve romantic affairs, sexual liaisons, pedophilic acts, and other sexual transgressions."[39] Sexual encounters can destroy a ministry and cause

---

[37] Norman L. Geisler, Christian Ethics: Contemporary Issues & Options (Grand Rapids, MI: Baker Publishing, 2010), 15.

[38] Scott B. Rae, Moral Choices: An Introduction to Ethics (Grand Rapids, MI: Zondervan, 1995), 319.

[39] Ibid., 15.

a lack of faith in the Church of God. Imagine a couple in the Church who had a twenty-four-year marriage. However, sometimes the appearance outside may differ from the reality inside the home. The couple appeared to have a solid foundation; however, the truth of the relationship almost destroyed the ministry. The man was a minister in the Church and had a good relationship with the youth. His wife was incredibly involved in working in the Church. The couple was successful in the development of a nursing home ministry every Saturday.

The Pastor noticed the minister became very relaxed about his responsibilities with the Church. He went from an individual who was faithful to the ministry; to becoming absent from the Church. The Pastor called the couple to discuss the matter. However, the minister remained silent about the truth. Finally, the wife met with the Pastor and explained that her husband was having an affair. The Pastors removed the minister from the pulpit and relieved him of his responsibilities in the Church. These actions caused great shock and disbelief within the Church. Some youths who looked up to this minister no longer wanted to participate in church activities. Some new members felt that the Church was no different from the world, and the nursing home ministry suffered from a lack of leadership.

Leaders' actions affect their ethical behavior and distract from the fundamental focus of God's Word. Leaders must understand the importance of professionalism—the truck stop is filled with many issues the leaders will face. However, as a leader, there must be an understanding of boundaries. "Michael Bayles outlines three central features that are necessary for an occupation to be professional; extensive training, a significant intellectual component in training, and a trained ability to provide an important service to society."[40]

Before an individual can evangelize, moral and ethical training is required. It is the leader's responsibility to administer ethical training to the group. This book will provide a training program to assist in developing an ethical training course. Ethical training is not a course taught once in a lifetime; it must be conducted yearly. It does not matter if it is a small or large church. Ethical training will assist in maintaining a professional church atmosphere. Many smaller churches in the communities—team up with other churches to develop an

---

[40] Ibid., 30.

ethical training program.

Ethical Training Outline

An ethical training outline must be prepared to organize the subjects covered. The outline provides the audience with an overview of the ethical class. The location must allow the interaction of the audience. I cannot stress the importance of understanding your audience. Ethical training is crucial to one's ministry. Therefore, the leader must construct an outline meeting/class to the audience's comprehension level. Below you will find a sample Ethical Training Outline:

ETHICAL TRAINING OUTLINE

1. Introduction

2. Code of Ethics

3. What is the Code of Ethics?

4. Why is the Code of Ethics training required?

5. Who needs Ethical Training Development?

6. The 5 Ethical Characteristics

7. Ethical Terminology

8. Biblical Views on ethics

9. Closing

Case Studies

An excellent ethical training program is having case studies so the group can interact in the class. Group interaction is a superb source to enhance knowledge of ethics. Leaders must remember these individuals communicate and assist others with life issues. Therefore, as many examples provided during the meeting, time limits are helpful to the program's success. Let us look at some case studies.

Case Study One

Cassandra has been assigned to the Truck Stop Ministry along with Deacon Wright for three weeks. During the daily visits, Cassandra noticed a woman coming to the area to see Deacon Wright. After a while, Deacon Wright begins to spend a lot of time with this woman. The second week at the Truck Stop Ministry, Cassandra noticed Deacon Wright coming out of a semi-truck with the woman, and they kissed before walking back to the area. As she watches, she understands there is a serious ethical issue. What should Cassandra do about the situation?

Case Study Two

After Cassandra remained assigned to the ministry for another two weeks, personal issues arose. However, she is committed to the ministry. She decides not to come to the truck stop on this day, leaving Deacon Mann alone at the ministry. On this day, a lady came who needed guidance. Although Deacon Mann lacked the proper training to assist the women, he went on and provided guidance. What ethical issues have arisen? What needs to happen to correct the situation? Is additional training necessary?

Throughout the years, there has been controversy about the need for biblical theology referenced in counseling. Specialists have challenged the necessity of Biblical counseling offered as professional support for others. The truck stop is filled with individuals in need of professional counseling. Therefore, a trained professional must be available to assist those challenged while working. Counseling takes time, and leaders of the Church have financial obligations worldwide. Therefore, the counselor must receive compensation for the job provided. Having a counselor on staff is essential. According to Lambert, "counseling is a theological discipline."[41]

---

[41] Heath Lambert, A Theology of Biblical Counseling; The Doctrinal Foundations of Counseling Ministry (Grand Rapids, MI: Zondervan, 2016), 11.

Some truck drivers have emotional issues. Counseling is an action many drivers need. Marital, depression, children, employment, and solitude are some drivers' issues. Some drivers require medications, while others remain focused on themselves to overcome the situation. Having a professional therapist is essential to the ministry.

Systematic Theology Counseling

Before an individual can gain a proper perspective of theological counseling, it is essential to define counseling. Lambert stated, "Counseling is a conversation where one party with questions, problems, and trouble seeks assistance from someone they believe had answers, solutions, and help."[42] The purpose is any counseling session is to assist the counselee in learning to deal with their life struggles. The Bible was written to provide humanity with examples of life on earth. Therefore, the teaching of the entire Bible is necessary for systematic theology.

Biblical Counseling Techniques

Biblical counseling requires the ability to interpret and translate the Scriptures. Therefore, anyone participating in the vision of understanding counseling practices. The ability to grasp the essential aspects of biblical doctrine. According to Lambert, "The authority of the Bible means that the Bible is our supreme standard for what we should believe and how we should behave because it comes from God, who cannot lie."[43] When counseling others, the person provides personal struggles; therefore, the counselor must seek directions. Christian counselors should have faith in God and seek guidance from God when counseling others.

God is love. Therefore, love should be displayed when counseling others. When individuals seek counseling from Christians, they watch their counselor's actions. The Bible will provide the message necessary to help the counselee. The counselor must have faith in the Bible. Trust that the Scripture will assist the person in

---

[42] Ibid., 13.

[43] Ibid., 36.

dealing with their struggles. Counseling is not just a counselor. People seek advice from non-professionals to understand how they should live. Christians have hope and faith in the Bible and the spiritual formation needed to recover.

Secular Counseling

Secular counseling is counseling without biblical references. This form of counseling reframes seeking the Word of God but relies on the person's ability to counsel. Many people obtain a degree in counseling. However, most of the information comes from book knowledge and theories. When guiding an individual, a person is dealing with the emotions of others. Therefore, a person must care in providing proper treatment. A secular counselor may fail to have a spiritual interest in the person, which is the non- appropriate information conveyed to the counselee.

Scripture Sufficiency

Lambert stated, "The doctrine of the sufficiency of Scripture is a promise that God himself will give you something from him to say in those sacred moments."[44] God is the only one who can provide the wisdom to share with another. "For the Lord gives wisdom, from his mouth come knowledge and understanding" (Prov. 2:6 KJV). Some believe that Biblical counseling should only be utilized when dealing with salvation. However, salvation helps a counselee's spiritual growth and faith when dealing with an addiction.

Common Grace

According to Lambert, "common grace is the good kindness of God that he shows to all people regardless of whether they have experienced the salvation that comes through Jesus Christ alone."[45] God displays grace to his creations. Humanity is born in sin and sometimes allows the flesh to lead their action. When this happens, God has grace. "Every person, whether a believer or an unbeliever

---

[44] Ibid., 38.

[45] Ibid., 67.

who has been ill, injured or in trouble and has recovered, been restored or rescued, has been saved by God in some temporal sense if not in the ultimate eternal sense."[46] God restores faith and belief in His will. Unbelievers are provided with the truth of the Scripture and knowledge of God's grace and mercy. Counseling can assist a person in dealing with the struggles of their daily lives. The goal is to help the person utilize their struggles while turning them into strengths versus weaknesses.

Christian Theology

Before one can believe in God, there must be knowledge of Christ. The counselor is instrumental in providing assignments that will assist the counselee in acquiring biblical knowledge. Many people struggle with understanding the ability of God and also the human side of God. Lambert stated, "Christians believe that Jesus is fully God and fully man-two distinct natures in one whole person."[47] Jesus was born of a virgin woman and began Christianity. Jesus is love; therefore, the salvation of humanity was His ultimate focus.

The Holy Spirit

The Holy Spirit was first introduced to humanity in Genesis. "Now the earth was formless and empty, darkness was over the surface of the deep, and the Spirit of God hovering over the waters" (Gen.1:2 KJV). The Spirit of God is present to comfort those seeking salvation. Therefore, biblical counseling is an essential part of a counselee's growth. However, receiving salvations and seeking God allows the Holy Spirit to work inside an individual's life. According to Lambert, "the Word of God is only effective when the Spirit of God renders it effective in the lives of individuals."[48]

The Holy Spirit dwells inside, providing direction that assists in the conviction of the world from sin. Therefore, a counselee will learn to develop a relationship with Christ. Having a relationship is through prayer and meditation. Biblical knowledge is essential in

---

[46] Ibid.

[47] Ibid., 138

[48] Ibid., 161.

gaining an understanding of the Word of God. The Spirit of God can change lives.

Theology of Counseling

Some people believe God is not needed in their lives; therefore, their knowledge of life's struggles becomes a gray area. However, the Bible was created to guide living while on earth. Every example of life struggle is displayed in the Bible. The significant part of the Bible, God's reactions, and punishments are in the Scriptures. Therefore, God has made His expectations known to humanity.

God Is Omnipresent

Biblical counseling can change a person's life. Instead of relying on secular ideas and theories, God introduces change. It is essential to know God. According to Lambert, when we know who God is, we also know that he is the most wonderful being in existence. Knowing who God is changing your life".[49] Having God in your life is a benefit; no longer are you alone in your deepest hours. God is always with you, regardless of the circumstance. Therefore, God is omnipresent, meaning; God is everywhere.

God Is Omnipotent

God is the creator of all things. "In the beginning, God created the heavens and earth" (Gen. 1:2 KJV). Since God created all things on earth, God knows the actions of the world. God created humanity and knew their struggles. Therefore, there is nothing a person cannot tell God. This action is known as omniscience.

God Is Omniscient

Humanity seeks knowledge. Sometimes while working through a situation, there are two paths to choose. The term is known as omniscient. God knows the paths of all humanity. The Church must understand the importance of counseling. Many members have

---

[49] Ibid., 104.

personal struggles that require professional guidance. The study will include some of the pertinent aspects of the chapters.

According to Lambert, "Jesus is an example of a biblical teacher who spent far more time counseling than he ever did preaching."[50] Leaders must spend an ample amount of time teaching. The teaching aspect happens during personal conversations with others. During these conversations, the leader begins a teach versus preach. The goal of anyone in the teaching profession is to communicate, so the student retains the information. Therefore, the counselor provides information in biblical counseling so the counselee will retain it.

Church Elders

Therefore, an elder must be a man whose life is above reproach. He must be faithful to his wife. He must exercise self-control, live wisely, and have a good reputation. He must enjoy having guests in his home, and he must be able to teach" (1 Tim. 3:2 NIV). The elders of the Church are essential to the teaching aspect of Biblical counseling. Elders are wise and have a relationship with God. Most Elders have worked in the Church and developed relationships with the other members. The members rely on the elder's wisdom and seek guidance in difficult situations.

Lambert continues to discuss, "The Bible clarifies that one important job of the pastor and elder is to lead the people in this church to grow in the task of counseling."[51] God has provided many in the Church with talents; teaching and counseling are talents. The goal of any Elder is to teach the truth of the Bible. Many wonder how education and counseling are similar or the same. When an individual needs counseling, teaching is essential in conveying the information.

Christian Community

The Christian community is also a significant part of biblical counseling. God is love; therefore, the member must learn to love and accept the challenges others face. The church congregation should

---

[50] Ibid., 306.

[51] Ibid., 307

remain on one accord. Therefore, when a member is struggling, the others display love and support for the individual. Relationship development is vital in the Church. The members must learn to trust each other. Trust is essential.

Professional Counseling

Churches should always have professional counselors available to assist with the guidance and challenges of members. Some are embarrassed to admit the need for a counselor; however, the world is born in sin. So, members will adjust and seek God for help with their challenges. At the same time, other members will require additional assistance in overcoming their struggles. Counseling is a daily occurrence, and churches should consider having a counselor on staff. However, the counselor must be trained.

Educational training is needed to enhance a person's ability in counseling. The education training aims to improve the counselors' knowledge of the laws associated with counseling. Some churches may not be able to have a counselor on staff. Thus, the churches can work together to provide counseling to the members.

Case Study One

John is a driver for JK Truck Driving company. John began his career five years ago and has enjoyed the ability to travel throughout the United States. In January 2020, the government announced that a pandemic had reached the United States, and the country is planning to shut down and only allow essential personnel to work. John understands he is considered vital and is required to work during the pandemic. John only takes $3 per mile per job; this amount covers his expenses and allows him to make a decent salary. During the pandemic, the amount paid per mile decreased, and most companies paid $1 per mile to truck drivers. John becomes extraordinarily depressed and confused. At the truck stop, John needs to speak with someone concerning his level of depression and seek encouragement. How can a truck stop ministry assist John?

Case Study Two

Khan just received information that Dan, his brother, is in the hospital, and the doctor is unsure about Dan's survival. Khan is in California delivering a load and is heading to the east coast. Khan immediately begins to travel east to get to the hospital. About two hundred miles from the hospital, Khan receives a phone call that Dan has passed. Khan was distraught and pulled into the truck stop to gain his composure. Khan knew it was not safe for him to drive in that condition. Khan needed someone to speak with to assist him in his grief. How can a truck stop ministry assist Khan?

Summary

This chapter provided several examples of biblical counseling that can be used in a truck stop ministry. Remember, these individuals are alone, and just because there are many trucks parted on the lot, everyone is a stranger. A ministry could provide a positive environment for the drivers. Chapter three provided letters about the struggle of addiction some drivers face. Drivers knowing that upon their arrival, someone will be present for them to speak with or provide services for fellowship. The driver can plan according to their time of worship. This chapter displays how valuable for churches to be involved in truck stop ministries.

Chapter Five

Understanding the Central Organ of the Body: The Brain

The brain is one of the central organs in the human body. Understanding the functions of the brain and the effects of addictions on the body is essential. Without the brain, the body would be unable to function. The body is dependent on the brain to signals to the other body part. According to Sorrentino and Remmert, the brain and the spinal cord make up the central nervous system.[1] The base of the brain is connected to the spinal cord, which allows the brain to control the body's mobility. The brain weight is around three pounds.[2]

The brain is covered by a hard shell known as the skull. Three additional layers protect the brain. The first layer is called the *dura mater,* and the next layer is known as the *arachnoid*, which is located in the middle, and the layer closer to the brain is the *pia mater*. Between the brain and the pia mater, there is the cerebrospinal fluid that assists with protecting the brain from any shock.[3] The brain is divided into three parts: the cerebrum, cerebellum, and brain stem.

> Sorrentino and Remmert stated that the cerebrum is the largest part of the brain. It is the center of thought and intelligence. The cerebrum is divided into two halves: the right and left hemispheres. The right hemisphere controls movement and the activities on the body's left side, while the left hemisphere controls the right side. The outside of the cerebrum is called the *cerebral cortex*. It controls the highest functions of the brain. These include reasoning, memory, consciousness, speech, voluntary muscle movement, vision, hearing, sensation, and other activities.[4]

---

[1] Sheila Sorrentino and Leighann Remmert, *Mosby's Textbook for Nursing Assistants* (St. Louis, MO: Elsevier, 2021), 118

[2] Ibid.

[3] Ibid.

[4] Ibid., 118.

Genesis 1:27 explains that God created man. Therefore, the development of man means that God created man inside and out. God provided man with a brain, which allowed man to have the ability to think and have choices. According to Sorrentino and Remmert,

> "The brain is made up of billions of neurons. Junctions between neurons, known as synapses, enable electrical and chemical messages to be transmitted from one neuron to the next in the brain, a process that underlies basic sensory functions and that is critical to learning, memory and thought formation, and other cognitive activities."[5]

However, what happens when drugs are introduced into the body? Let's begin with alcohol consumption. Alcohol is a liquid drug that affects a person's central nervous system.

> "Sorrentino and Remmert continue to discuss that the human nervous system conducts stimuli from sensory receptors to the brain and spinal cord and sends impulses back to other body parts. As with other high vertebrates, the human nervous system has two major parts: the central nervous system and the peripheral nervous system (the nerves that carry impulses to and from the central nervous system). In humans, the brain is especially large and well developed".[6]

When a drug effect the body/brain, it is called intoxication. When a person is intoxicated, they lose control of their ability to control their bodily functions. In the transportation industry, drivers need to maintain control of their functions. If a driver is intoxicated, driving is dangerous, affecting the driver and the public. According to Sorrentino and Remmert.

> "Alcohol belongs in the class with barbiturates, minor tranquilizers, and general anesthetics, and it is commonly classified as a depressant. The effects of alcohol on the brain is rather paradoxical. Under some behavioral conditions, alcohol

---

[5] Ibid.

[6] Ibid.

can serve as an excitant, and under other conditions, as a sedative. At very high concentrations, it acts increasingly as a depressant, leading to sedation, stupor, and coma. The excitement phase exhibits the well-known signs of exhilaration, loss of socially expected restraints, loquaciousness, unexpected changes in mood, and unmodulated anger. Excitement may actually be caused indirectly or by the effect of alcohol in suppressing inhibitory centres of the brain than by direct stimulation of the manifested behavior. The physical sign of exciting intoxication is slurred speech, unsteady gait, disturbed sensory perceptions, and inability to make fine motor movements. Again, these effects are produced not by the direct action of alcohol on the misbehaving and senses but by itself its effects on the brain centres that control muscle activity.

The most important immediate action of alcohol is on the higher functions of the brain-those of thinking, learning, remembering, and making judgments. Many of the alleged salutary effects of alcohol on performance (such as better dancing, happier moods, sounder sleeping, less sexual inhibition, and greater creativity) have been shown in controlled experiments to be a function of suggestion and subjective assessment. In reality, alcohol improves performance only through muscles, relaxation, and guilt reduction or loss of social inhibition."[7]

When alcohol enters the body, the alcohol begins to travel throughout the bloodstream and causes brain activities to slow down, causing the body to become impaired.

Alcohol changes a person's thinking, which is considered a mind-altering drug. "According to Sorrentino and Remmert, the prefrontal cortex of the brain is the area that tells the body what is needed for its survival."[8] For example, if the body needs food, the prefrontal cortex communicates to the body, alerting the person it is time to eat. Within the prefrontal cortex, the mesolimbic dopamine

---

[7] Ibid.

[8] Chuck Smith and Jason Hunt, *Understanding Addiction, Know Science, No stigma* (Visualize Publishing, 2021), 27-28.

communicates to the body when a person has eaten, and the body is full. Dopamine is essential in understanding the cravings one may feel when one is addicted to drugs. When a person faces drug addiction, satisfying the dopamine is challenging for an addict.

Mind-altering substances artificially increase the level of dopamine significantly.[9] As people introduce abused substances into their bodies, the body begins to change. The mind tells the body that this new substance is needed for the body to function. "The brain doesn't recognize these substances as dangerous. The brain feels the artificial bump and gets fooled into thinking it is real; that is just like food and water, its necessary to survive."[10]

According to Drs. Smith and Hunt, addiction represents a faulty braking system in a car. When a person is driving a car, and the braking system begins to malfunction, the person driving the car can't stop. The same actions happen when a person is on drugs.

The mind believes that for the body to function properly, it needs drugs. Therefore, the mind prevents the person from overcoming the cravings one is facing. One must look at the symptoms of addiction: "compulsive behavior, the loss of control, the constant cravings. And one likely doesn't need us to recount the consequences, the inability to recognize behavioral problems, to comprehend the effects of one's interpersonal relationships, the relapse, and remissions."[11]

Once the brain's receptors recognize the substance and the person continues to use the drug for a long time, the brain is addicted and relates the information to the body. "For the person addicted, he needs more and more of what he's addicted to assist in getting over the craving bump, to overcome the restless, irritable discontent."[12] This action allows the addiction to take over and control the addict's ability to function. "Eventually, people with substance use disorder are no longer looking for pleasure. They're looking to feel normal."[13]

Many people's addictions begin with seeking a way to overcome

---

[9] Ibid., 30.

[10] Ibid.,31.

[11] Ibid., 31.

[12] Ibid., 33.

[13] Ibid., 34.

pain. Analgesics are drugs that assist in relieving pain. Depending on the pain level, a person can become dependent on the drug. According to Sorrentino and Remmert,

"Several commonly used natural or synthetic derivatives of morphine are used in drug therapeutics. Codine, a naturally occurring opium alkaloid that can be made synthetically, is a proper oral analgesic, primarily when used with aspirin.

Meperidine was an early synthetic analog of morphine, marketed under the trade name Demerol. It was initially thought to be able to provide significant short- lasting analgesia and little or no addiction because of its shortened duration of action; however, this belief proved false. Methadone, a synthetic opioid analgesic, has a long-lasting analgesic effect when taken orally and is used to moderate withdrawal effects from heroin addiction. Among the opioid antagonist drugs, naloxone and its longer-lasting orally active version, naltrexone, are used primarily to reverse morphine overdoses and reverse the chemical stupor of various causes, including alcohol intoxication and anesthesia."[14]

As the brain continues to function and new drugs enter the body, opioids display a need to overcome the craving. Some of the symptoms of withdrawal are anxiety and tremors. Therefore, the brain tells the body that to overcome this feeling, the body needs an opioid. By the individual increasing the substance, the body begins to reject it, causing a person to become unconscious. This action is known as a drug overdose.

A drug overdose is one of the most dangerous parts of addiction. At the time of an overdose, the body is shutting down because it has been over-stimulated by the drug.

During this time, it is essential that the professional attempt to remove the substance from the person's body, reducing the amount of the drug flowing through one's bloodstream.

As the brain attempts to cope with the trauma, some individuals cannot withstand the substance. When the brain shuts down, the other organs begin to shut down, leading to death. Brain death is the irreversible destruction of the brain. "Before the invention of life-support systems, brain death always led quickly to death of the body."[15]

---

[14] Ibid.

[15] Ibid.

The brain can be described as a computer. When the computer stops working, the electricity cannot flow through the computer. All other components of the computer die, losing all data. The same happens in the brain. Without the brain, nothing is present to send signals to the other parts of the body

Summary

Before a person can engage in biblical counseling, one must understand the body's anatomy. The brain is the central part of the body, which sends signals to other areas, reminding the individual of the body's needs. Working in a truck stop ministry, one should clearly understand the consequences of drugs. When a person is addicted to drugs, they are changing the chemical makeup of their body. Introducing their body to a substance could trigger the mind to believe that it would not have all the nutrients needed to remain healthy. However, during this process, the individual is actually destroying the body's essential functions.

This chapter provided an understanding of the parts of the brain and the area that control the impulses sent throughout the body. One of the great reminders is that Smith and Hunt described an addict as a failing braking system in a vehicle. The car won't stop. The addict can't stop. Biblical counseling is essential due to a person needs to learn how to reframe from the use of drugs. The Bible has provided many examples of the power of God to guide a person through an illness.

Truck driver who suffers from addiction need spiritual guidance to help them fight it. Having a ministry in the truck stops would allow the drivers to communicate their struggles with a professional who can assist them in realizing they have the ability to overcome the addiction. Addiction is in mind. Just as a person has to study to retrain their mind, the same process is necessary for an addict. An addict must develop a relationship with God, where on the night when they are alone in the truck, instead of seeking a drug dealer, the person will seek guidance from God.

Chapter Six
Drug Addictions

The purpose of this chapter is to provide information on many addictive drugs. While working in a truck stop ministry, drivers face addictions. Professional biblical counselors working in a truck stop ministry must be knowledgeable about addictive drugs. This chapter can assist in understanding what harm drugs can do to the human body. Drugs affect the body in different ways. However, some of the drugs in this project are not harmful. It is the abuse of the drug that causes a person to become addicted. Mitch Earleywine wrote an incredibly detailed book about marijuana. Although medical marijuana will be discussed later in the chapter, according to Earleywine, "smoked cannabis clearly helps some problems and may cost less than other medications."[16]

This chapter will focus on the drugs introduced to the body for recreational use.

Marijuana, Cocaine, meth, heroin opioids are all addictive drugs that have affected society. The drug, throughout continuous use, begins to devour the person. First Peter 5:8 reminds Christians that it is vital to "be sober, be vigilant; because your adversary the devil, as a roaring lion walketh about, seeking whom he may devour." Therefore, this scripture explains the importance of biblical counseling to help individuals understand their purpose and have faith in God. 1 Peter 5:7 reminds Christians to "cast all your care upon him; for he careth for you." The truck stop ministry is vital in helping drivers suffering from addiction understand that there are options other than drug addictions.

Marijuana

Another name for marijuana is cannabis. Before one can understand the effects of marijuana, it is essential to look at the history of cannabis. According to Earleywine,

---

[16] Mitch Earleywine, Understanding Marijuana: A new Look at the Scientific Evidence (New York, NY: Oxford University, 2002), 167.

"Unlike most plants that provide drugs, hemp provides dozens of products. None of these items contains meaningful amounts of tetrahydrocannabinol, (THC), the primary psychoactive ingredient in marijuana. In contrast to psychoactive cannabis plants, which contain 2% YHC or more, industrial help often contains as little as 15% THC. Hemp provides fiber, cloth, paper, and food, as well as soaps, shampoos, and oil. People grew hemp widely for these industrials use which helped the plant spread from Asia through India, Africa, Europe, and the Americans."[17]

There the marijuana plant, if used correctly, has been an essential part of society, providing many of the basic needs of humanity. This plant has provided so many of the essentials for society. How could this become an addictive drug?

In and around 2737 B.C., began the medicinal use of marijuana.[18] Society began to learn that the hemp found in the marijuana plant posed a healing factor. According to Earlywine,

"The cannabis plant's history as a source of hemp is separated from its story of medicine. Cannabis's use as a treatment for a variety of illnesses which helped it spread from ancient Asia throughout the world. The plant consistently appeared in pharmacopeia and folk medicine as a treatment for pain, seizures, muscle spasms, poor appetite, nausea, insomnia, asthma, and depression. Its potential to alleviate labor pains, premenstrual symptoms, and menstrual cramps also received attention in multiple medical reports from ancient times to the present.

Marijuana's possible medical applications have continued to increase its popularity, even with individuals who would frown upon recreational use. Therapeutic cannabis has also provided intriguing scientific and legal research."[19]

---

[17] Ibid., 4.

[18] Ibid., 9.

[19] Ibid.

According to the Center of Disease Control and Prevention (CDC), marijuana is the most commonly used federally illegal drug in the United States. Recent research estimated that approximately three in ten people who use marijuana have marijuana use disorders.[20] The truck stop ministry is beneficial in providing counseling for those who are suffering from marijuana addiction. The CDC also provides statistical data that forty-eight million people used the drug in 2019.[21] In 2012 the States of Colorado and Washington became the first states to legalize the recreational use of marijuana.

Cocaine Erythroxylon Coca

The Erythroxylon caca was discovered when the Spaniards migrated to Peru.

According to Platt, "they found the inhabitants continually chewing on a combination of leaves and ash, which resulted, its users claimed, in increased strength and endurance.

The plant resembles tea leaves."[22] As the plant began to spread worldwide, scientists began finding different coca plant uses.

According to Platt, using the coca leaves, coca lozenges, Bordeaux wine, alkali, and two ounces of fresh coca leaves created Vin Martani and coca wine. It was touted as a cure for catarrh, and patent medicines containing cocaine abound. The coca leaf was also used for cigarettes and syrups. Later the leave was said to help people suffering from hay fever and asthma. By putting 420 mg of cocaine in the nasal cavity, the cocaine would cause complete absorption.[23]

At an annual meeting of the American Medical Association in 1894, the effects of Cocaine were discussed.

"We know the great value of the drug (cocaine) when properly used. The peculiarity delighted effect it seems to have upon

---

[20] Center of Disease Control and Prevention, Marijuana and Public Health,
https://wwwicdc.gov/marijuana/gov, 8/30/2022..

[21] Ibid.

[22] Jerome Platt, *Cocaine Addiction Theory, Research, and Treatment* (Cambridge, MA: Harvard University, 1997), 3.

[23] Ibid.,5.

many persons and the baleful effects which have followed it over the use. Is it not time, that part been the cause of this state of things, should give our attention to the subject. Cocaine, one of the most valuable drugs, can be more harmful than alcohol and opium. The use of cocaine is increasing to a severe extent. For this, the medical professional is largely responsible. It is the duty of the professional to guard the public by every proper means against the dangers arising from the use of cocaine.[24]

Many times, additives are used in different products to increase their strength and encourage the consumer to purchase them. Many may wonder how the soda Coke got the name Coca-Cola. According to Platt, cocaine was used in the drink. 4.5 mg of cocaine was used in a six-ounce bottle of Coke. The process continued until 1990 when the coke formula was changed.[25] According to the Britannica Encyclopedia,

> "The prolonged or compulsive use of cocaine in any of the purified forms can cause severe personality disturbance, inability to sleep, and loss of appetite. A toxic psychosis can develop involving paranoid delusions and disturbing tactile hallucinations in which the user feels insects crawling under his skin. Cocaine abuse, which had been a marginal drug problem throughout much of the 20th century, grew alarmingly in the late 20th century in several counties. Cocaine had become responsible for a markedly increased proportion of drug-induced deaths."[26]

There are many forms of an addictive drugs that will continue to affect the brain's ability to function without the drug notated in chapter five. According to Platt, "cocaine is variously known as C, blow, flake, versus boy. Nose candy, paradise, snow, stardust, toot, white lady. Knowing and understanding the terminology is essential to

---

[24] Ibid., 7-8.

[25] Ibid.

[26] Britannica Encyclopedia, Cocaine, http//britannicaencyclopdia/cocaine, 8/30/2022.

a person working in a truck stop ministry. Any form of this type of drug can impair a driver's ability to operate the truck properly. Therefore, providing information and counseling to those who suffer from cocaine addiction is vital. Respondent three suffered from cocaine addiction. The respondent's three difficulties ranged from the loss of time, stealing, high usage of money, and vehicle accident. Therefore, the truck stop ministry and the trained counselor could provide the help some drivers need.

Alcohol

Alcohol is one of the addictive substances that is sold at many truck stops or within the surrounding area. Alcohol was developed in early societies. The Britannica Encyclopedia states, "alcohol is the oldest and still one of the most widely used drugs."[27] According to the Britannica Encyclopedia,

> "The origin of alcoholic beverages is lost in the midst of prehistory. Fermentation can occur in any mashed sugar-containing food, such as grapes, grains, berries, or honey which is left exposed to warm air. Yeasts from the air act on the sugar, converting it to alcohol and carbon dioxide. Alcoholic beverages were thus probably discovered accidentally by pre-agriculture cultures. Early people presumably liked the effects, not the taste, and proceeded to purposeful production. From merely gathering the wild growing raw materials, they went on to regular cultivation of the vine and other suitable crops."[28]

As the world continued to evolve, society began to realize that there are multiple uses for the alcoholic beverage. According to the Britannica Encyclopedia, "alcoholic beverages have a nutritional value. Second, they were the best medicine available for some illnesses, especially for relieving pain. Also, they facilitated religious ecstasy and communion."[29]

---

[27] Mark Keller and George Vaillant, *Alcohol Consumption*. Britannica Encyclopedia, http//britannicaencyclopdia/alcoholconsumption/, 5, 8/30/2022.

[28] Ibid.

[29] Ibid., 6.

The gain and ingredients used to make liquor could be helpful for humans. But people will often continue to abuse and refrain from ingesting the proper amount of liquor. According to Collins, the Bible does not teach people to abstain from liquor but mentions temperance.[30] Wine is discussed in the Bible. The Last Supper is an example of wine being used as a celebration, and Jesus drinks from the cup of wine. However, one must reframe from allowing liquor to prevent a person from functioning in society.

Galatians 5:19-21 and Ephesians 5:18 both remind Christians that drinking to the point of drunkenness is not of God.

There are several effects when a person abuses alcohol. It is essential to remember that alcohol abuse is a toxin in the body. According to the Britannica Encyclopedia,

> "In the ingestion of an alcoholic beverage, the alcohol is rapidly absorbed in the gastrointestinal tract (stomach and intestines) because it does not undergo any digestive processes; thus, alcohol rises to high levels in the blood in a relatively short time. From the blood, the alcohol is distributed to all parts of the body and has an especially pronounced effect on the brain, on which it exerts a depressant action under the influence of alcohol; the functions of the brain and depressed in a characteristic pattern. The most complex actions of the brain, judgment, self- criticism, and the inhibitions learned from earliest childhood are depressed first, and the loss of control results in a feeling of excitement in the early stages. Under the influence of increasing amounts of alcohol, the drinker gradually becomes less alert, awareness of his environment becomes dim and hazy, muscular coordination deteriorates, and sleep is facilitated."[31]

With the substance readily available to the drivers, having a truck stop ministry in the truck stop would help offer another option. Chapter four discussed deontological and unitarian views of society. However, it is essential to look at how these views describe addictions.

---

[30] Gary Collins, *Christian Counseling A Comprehensive Guide* (Nashville, TN: Thomas Nelson, 2007), 659.

[31] Ibid.

According to Smith and Hunt, "in our society, alcohol isn't just socially acceptable, its socially expected."[32]

Methamphetamine

Methamphetamine is also known as d-deoxyephedrine.[33] Like all the other substances discussed in this chapter, all have had some form of positive use on the human body. Many medical professionals used this drug for several forms of treatment. "Methamphetamines are prescribed to treat certain medical conditions, including attention-deficit/hyperactivity disorder (ADHD), narcolepsy, and obesity. In the United States, it is marketed under the brand name Desoxyn.[34] Some of the behavior difference is alleviated depression, fatigue, hyperkinetic behavior disturbances of children, postencephalitic parkinsonism, enuresis, nausea during pregnancy, and obesity.[35]

Many surveys were conducted throughout the years to gain a perspective on the drug. The Britannica Encyclopedia states that a

"Group of 492 addicts who had been institutionalized showed a fourteen percent rate of chronic psychosis with evidence of permanent organic brain damage. In the language of the streets, "Meth is Death." The amphetamines produce habituation, drug dependency, physiological tolerance, and toxic effect, but no physical addiction."

This drug is still considered an addictive drug which affects the ability of some to function in society.

Heroin and Opium

Heroin and opium are drugs used for psychotropic versus medical use.[36] The native society used this drug in the Western Hemisphere from plants that contained hallucinogenic substances.

---

[32] Chuck Smith and Jason Hunt, *Understanding Addiction, Know Science No Stigma* (Orlando, Fl: Visualize, 2021), 78.

[33] Ibid.

[34] Ibid.

[35] Britannica Encyclopedia, Drug Use, http://britannicaencyclopedia/druguse/amphetamines. 18, 8/30/2022.

[36] Ibid., 1.

These drugs were mainly made for scared mushrooms from Mexico.[37] The Native Americans used the drug to increase their religious experiences. However, because of the serve physiological and psychological affect, the government regulated the use of these drugs. According to the Britannia Encyclopedia,

> "It is suggested that drug use can represent a primitive search for euphoria and expression of prohibited infantile craving or the release of hostility and contempt; the measure of self-destruction that follows can constitute punishment and the act of expiation. It has also been suggested that this type of drug use will be strongly influenced by the individual characteristic way of relating to the world."[38]

When researching the psychotropic drug and looking at the history of opiates, one will learn that the drug is from the poppy. This drug is a narcotic and was used to help induce sleep. However, as one has learned during the research. The main issue results from individuals using drugs beyond the allowed limits. Some of the effects include nausea, vomiting, constipation, itchiness of the facial region, yawning, sweating, flushing of the skin, a warm sensation in the stomach, a fall in the body's temperature, and diminished respiration.[39]

Summary

This chapter aims to provide insight into the effects of the drugs. The chapter supports the need for a truck stop ministry. When reviewing the drugs, one can see that the issue in many examples is not the drug. The problem is individual abuse of the drug. When the drug is abused, the person suffers the risk of becoming addicted to the drug. As stated in chapter five, the drugs affect the brain, which sends a signal to the other areas of the body. Once a new substance has been introduced to the body significantly, the body believes that the drug is needed for survival. Having trained individuals in the truck stop

---

[37] Ibid.

[38] Ibid., 6

[39] Ibid., 11.

ministry can assist with providing accurate information and guiding an addict to understanding the damage that drug use can cause to their system.

Chapter Seven
Brain Addictions

The purpose of this chapter is to assist the reader in understanding the issues drivers face once becoming addicted to the Internet. As the world continued to evolve, many different forms of communication were developed. In the 1980s phones were used just as a form of communication verbally from one person to another. Now phones have many uses and platforms that will cause a person to become addicted to the device. Social media continues to capture the interest of many. Truck drivers become isolated in their trucks many times. This isolation can cause a person to find an object or source to occupy their time.

 The dissertation is not implying that the Internet is not needed in society. However, the focus is on how the Internet can provide options for drivers to prevent them from becoming addicted. This chapter discusses television, the internet, social media, and gaming systems. This chapter will also discuss how people become addicted. Before a person can gain an actual perspective of brain addiction, it is essential to look at information from an addict and information from specialists.

 Cheryl Pawlowski wrote a book that addresses addiction called *Glued to the Tube*. The book addresses the threat of television in society today. Now other electronic devices contain the same electronic circuits as a television, and televisions can now connect to the Internet. Drivers no longer have to sit in the drivers' lounge to look at television. The television and electronic devices are present in the truck. This action causes the driver to become isolated. According to Pawlowski,

> "Taking control of the information obtained from and used social media and television sites is crucial. "If you hold specific religious beliefs, consider joining a church or synagogue, and make participation a priority. It's important that you understand the full doctrine of your chosen faith. Also, look for ways you can incorporate the values of your faith into everyday activities."[1]

---

[1] Cheryl Pawlowski, *Glued to the Tube The Threat of Television Addiction of*

It was essential for scientists to develop images that would stimulate the brains of humans, which encouraged them to continue watching a particular source. The television, internet, social media, and gaming systems contain the same human perception form, drawing the brain to a particular source. According to the Britannia Encyclopedia,

> "A television system must be designed to embrace the essential capabilities of these senses, particularly the sense of vision. The aspect of vision that must be considered includes the ability of the human eye to distinguish the brightness, colors, details, sizes, shapes, and positions of objects in a scene before it. Aspects of hearing include the ability of the ear to distinguish the pitch, loudness, and distribution of sound. Television technology must deal with the fact that the human vision employs hundreds and thousands of separate electrical circuits located in the optic nerve running from the retina to the brain in order to convey simultaneously in two dimensions the whole content of the scene on which the eye focused."[2]

Respondent Eight

During Respondent Eight's ten years of driving a truck, many changes have happened in the trucking industry and technology. For this survey, Respondent Eight wanted to be known as Lady A. Lady A is a solo truck driver. Most of the time, I stay in the truck. Working in a male-dominated industry, there are limited activities for women. I found myself focusing on television and other electronic devices to occupy my downtime. Sometimes I would watch television all day from one series to another. If I became bored with the television shows, I would revert to social media. I even found myself playing games on the Internet. After years of this action, I realized I was addicted to television and similar devices. Having a truck stop ministry available to the truck driver would allow drivers to fellowship with

---

Today's Family (Nashville: TN: Sourcebook, 2000), 201.

[2] Ibid.

others. It would also be nice to have a way to communicate with the church via social media.

Comments and Supporting Data of Respondent Eight

Respondent Eight provided a great example of the need for a truck stop ministry.

This ministry would help the drivers by removing them from the world's actions and providing an option. As stated in the previous chapter, many of these men and women travel alone in their trucks. Being able to fellowship with others is a significant change to a driver's routine. Social media has opened the door to expanding communication between the world and the church.

Chapter one explained that truck drivers are transit individuals. Therefore, a database must be developed to allow drivers to communicate with those they have met. According to Jones, "while a social media plan primarily focuses on sharing content to get likes, comments, and shares, a social ministry strategy focuses on building relationships and facilitating connections between and among people so that discipleship can happen. Relationships are the foundation for discipleship."[3]

Summary

The internet is an essential part of the truck stop ministry. The focus is to develop a relationship that could lead to discipleship. Introducing the internet into this dissertation is to remind the churches that communication does not stop at the truck stop. Ongoing communication is essential to building relationships. Although Respondent Eight discussed being addicted to the internet and television, the ministry could provide other options for the drivers to review.

---

[3] Nona Jones, *From Social Media to Social Ministry A Guide to Digital Discipleship* (Grand Rapids, MI: Zondervan, 2020), 25.

Chapter Eight
Body Addictions

This chapter examines the research concerning a person's body dealing with addictions. Although all addictions are a part of the body, sexual desires, and obesity addictions are essential parts of one's body addictions. This chapter will provide information on obesity, which is considered an epidemic. A book by Zoe Harcombe, *The Obesity Epidemic*, explains the challenges of being overweight. This chapter will also address sexual desires when working away from home. According to Welch, "sex and food have been common since biblical times. By our outward appearances, they are problems begging for a response of self-control. Yet even though it appears to be the perfect antidote, self-control is not always part of the addiction discussion."[1] Second Timothy 1:7 reminds Christians that God has provided power to overcome the temptations of the world. However, one must take control of their addiction and reframe from allowing temptation to manifest.

Obesity

Many drivers suffer from body addictions. Chapter nine will provide additional information on the truck body and the amenities inside the truck. However, most trucks lack the ability for the drivers to prepare their food. Most drivers are forced to eat processed food or at restaurants; therefore, many foods lack the nutritional value needed for healthy eating. According to the Britannica Encyclopedia,

> "Obesity, also called corpulence or fatness, is excessive accumulation of body fat, usually by consuming more calories than the body can use. The excess calories are then stored as fat or adipose tissue. Overweight, if moderate, is not necessarily obesity, particularly in muscular or large-boned individuals."[2]

---

[1] Edward Welch, Addictions A Banquet in the Grave (Phillipsburg, NJ: P & R, 2001), 201.

[2] Britannia Encyclopedia, Obesity, Http://britanniaencyclopedia/obesity/

One must first understand the struggles drivers face while on the road. Drivers drive ten to eleven hours a day per DOT regulations. During this process, the drivers sit most of the day, which limits the driver's ability to exercise. Along with the lack of exercise and the nutritional value of the food, in most cases, drivers become obese. According to Harcombe,

> "There are two forms of fat in the human body; triglycerides and fatty acids. Human fat (adipose tissue) is stored as triglycerides, and fatty acids are burned for fuel. Triglycerides are three fatty acids bound together on the backbone of glycerol. Fat centers and exits fat cells as acids triglycerides are too big to move across the cells membranes."[3]

In some cases, obesity is a genetic trait. Some issues are based on a person's genetic makeup, while others suffer from the cultural diet. According to the Britannica Encyclopedia documented that the "World Health Organization (WHO), which considered global obesity an epidemic, in 2016 more than 1.9 billion adults (age 18 or older) worldwide were overweight and 650 million, representing 13 percent of the world's adult population, were obese. The truck stop ministry could help suggest healthy foods that can be purchased at the truck stops or food that can be purchased at the grocery with low-fat content.

> According to the Britannica Encyclopedia, "obesity is traditionally defined as an increase in body weight that was greater than twenty percent of an individual's ideal body weight. Weight is associated with the lowest risk of death, as determined by certain factors, such as age, height, and gender. Based on these factors, being overweight could then be defined as a fifteen to twenty percent increase over their ideal body weight. However, today the definition of overweight and

---

1.

[3] Zoe Harcombe, The Obesity Epidemic (Britain: Columbia, 2015), 15.

obesity are based primarily on measures of height and weight, not mobility. These measures are used to calculate body mass index, a person's BMI. This number is central to determining whether an individual is clinically defined as obese."[4]

Proper eating habits are essential to maintaining a healthy body. A ministry that helps guide drivers to appropriate eating habits is vital. Every two years, drivers must take a physical to determine their physical health to operate a commercial vehicle. The DOT- required physical will be discussed in chapter nine. If a driver is deemed unhealthy, their license can be suspended. These actions will lead to a loss of income and employment. A truck stop ministry would assist in helping drivers suffering from this addiction. A trained nutritionist would open communication with the drivers, helping them understand the importance of healthy eating.

Sexual Desires

Sexual desire is an action that began with Adam and Eve. Genesis 4:1 states that Adam knew his wife and that she became pregnant with Cain. Genesis 1:28 explains that the purpose of the relationship between Adam and Eve was to go forth and have children to assist in populating the earth. Sex was initially developed to continue the creation of humanity. However, just as with any addiction, the action stems from a person not controlling their actions.

According to Collins, "sexuality, like everything else created, has fallen into trouble. We are more vulnerable than ever, living in a society where crowds of sexual innuendoes are in every available space, whether billboards or office conversations."[5] The actions happen in the truck stops. Some offer pornography magazines, as well as sexual pleasure stores, are located near a truck stop. Collins stated, "that which God created for our enjoyment and intimacy has become perverted." Sexual perversion has become the prominent example of sin and other measures of unhealthy sexuality."[6] The truck stop

---

[4] Ibid.

[5] Gary Collins, *Christian Counseling, A Comprehensive Guide* (Nashville, TN: Thomas Nelson, 2007), 339

[6] Ibid.,340.

ministry would be beneficial in helping men and women deal with their sexual desires while away from home.

Summary

This chapter discusses both sexual and obesity addictions which are faced within the truck stop. The Bible reminds Christians of the importance of reframing from the world's temptations. Proverbs 1:10 tells a Christian that if you are tempted, do not allow yourself to be overcome by temptation.

"At the same time, don't be afraid to help addicts take responsibility for their choices. Disabusing people of shame doesn't mean denying the reality that they have made poor choices or done bad things while under the influence, nor does it mean shielding people from the consequences of their actions."[7]

As a leader, there must not be a disconnect between addressing sin and helping those with addictions. The purpose of the church is to spread the Gospel and increase discipleship within the church body and doing so may require the development of ministry outside the four walls of the church. Truck drivers face these addictions regularly and having a ministry within the truck stop would assist in helping drivers understand and deal with these addictions.

---

[7] Jonathan Benz, *The Recovery Minded Church Loving and Ministering to People with Addiction* (Downers Grove, IL: IVP Books, 2006), 120.

Chapter Nine
Trucking Industry

The transportation industry began in the later 1800s. Before an individual or group can engage in ministry, it is vital to understand the community's history and needs. The transportation industry is essential for the growth of the global economy. The transportation of goods is by air, water, and land. However, even though these methods offer a safe form of transportation, the goods must reach seaports, airports, and warehousing facilities. The goods are then transported to the stores for consumption by the American people. "Now, there's one industry that ensures that American people get the bulk of what they consume. And it currently transports over 72% of the freight in the U.S."[1] The supplies must still get to the consumer. Therefore, drivers operated smaller vehicles known as semis and trailers to ensure the goods reached the proper location.

This chapter will provide a history of the transportation industry. The information focuses on truck driving; however, other transportation options may be necessary to gain a complete perspective—understanding the industry, the requirements, and state law.

One of the essential aspects of a ministry is gaining an appreciation for the group. The chapter provides clarity on the community and spiritual needs. The Bible supports the importance of a community. Romans 12:4-5 expresses the importance of the body and that one body works together.

Current Regulatory Requirements

Before a person can take the required examination, a driver must take a physical examination.[2] The examination aims to ensure that a driver is physically fit to operate a commercial vehicle.[3] Depending on the condition of the drivers, the drivers are given a two-year medical

---

[1] Clement Harrison, Trucking Business (Nashville: TN: Harrison, 2020), 5.

[2] Thomas Francs, Trucker's Guide for Beginning Truck Drivers (Meadville, PA: Fulton Books, 2021), 42.

[3] Ibid.

certificate.[4] This medical certificate must remain in the driver's possession while operating a commercial vehicle. The medical certificate is sent via email or fax to the State where the driver is licensed. The State must prove that the driver has met all requirements before operating a commercial vehicle.

Current regulations limit the ability of the truck driver to operate a commercial vehicle. For an individual to legally operate a commercial vehicle, they must be 21 years old. The person must attend a driving school. The individual must first take a written examination, and upon passing the test, the individual will receive a learner's permit.

Upon completing the school, the next portion of the test consists of two parts; part one is considered a walk-around. The potential licensee and a licensed commercial examiner are present for the test. During this process, the licensee must name every component of the vehicle. A truck driver must have extensive knowledge of the operation of the semi. This process is called a pre-trip. The driver must complete the pre-trip daily before driving the vehicle. The purpose of this process is to ensure the truck is road ready. This process is a Department of Transportation (DOT) regulation.

The second part of the test consists of a driving examination. The examiner provides direction to the driver and tests the skills and maneuverability of the semi. The test focuses on the ability to drive, park, shift, and properly turn the vehicle. After completing this process and passing all exams, the individual receives a commercial driver's license, making the individual eligible to drive and work for a transportation company. Some areas require the drivers to have unique identification when entering seaports and rail yards.

Truck Requirement

Unless a special permit is issued, a truck cannot weigh over 80,000 lbs, which includes truck, trailer, and freight. The semi-truck has three rows of tires, and each row is called an axel. The semi-truck axles in the rear cannot weigh more than 34,000 lbs. when transporting goods. The trailer has two axles, which can also carry 34,000 lbs. The axles assist with the weight distribution of the shipment. Trailers over the weight could cause extreme damage to the vehicle and wear and

---

[4] Ibid.

tear to the roads.

Therefore, the government authorities developed weight stations on the highway to check the weight of the semi. Once the driver has loaded their trucks at the warehousing facilities, the driver then, in many cases, will proceed to the scale to ensure the weight requirements are met. The highways are equipped with weight stations, and the DOT is present to ensure the weights are correct with the goods the driver carries.

Many semi-trucks contain an onboard device that informs the truck driver if entry into the weight station is necessary. Any overweight trucks remain subjected to fines, and the trailer must be at the proper weight so the driver can continue their journey. Therefore, the truck stop contains a CAT scale used to obtain the truck's weight before the driver begins transporting the goods on the highway. This process allows the driver and the company to distribute the weight properly before entering a weight station.

The truck and trailer must have an inspection once a year. The inspection checks the functioning of the semi and trailer to ensure the vehicle is safe to drive. Some companies require inspections multiple times a year. The maintenance of a truck is costly and requires long periods. During this time, the drivers must stay in hotels until the completion of repairs.

Many businesses try to support truck drivers when repairs require them to seek other options for their basic survival needs. Hotels offer discounts for stranded drivers. Some organizations make welcome packages for stranded drivers, while others provide transportation to and from the hotel to assist the drivers. However, where is the Church? There are many forms of support for the drivers who continue to support the local community—stranded drivers need basic survival needs. One could ask the question of how the Church can offer support, and the Church could prepare an informational pamphlet that provides specific contacts supporting the needs of stranded truck drivers.

Types of Trucks

There are several styles of trucks. Understanding the setup is essential to understanding the driver's needs. Most trucks have two seats in the front and two beds in the back. "Sleeping in the cab of the truck is almost necessary to make a living being a trucker."[5] The truck may have a television and microwave depending on the style.

However, some trucks are not equipped with the power to run the devices without the proper equipment. At the same time, other trucks are set up with an alternate power source known as an APU. This device allows the vehicle to operate when the diesel engine is not running. Different devices in the truck can function without causing the truck's batteries to fail. The other device equipped in some trucks is a generator. The generator is a more robust power source that again allows other devices to operate in the vehicle. Generators are typically used in semi-trucks with large refrigerators and stoves built into the cabinets.

One may ask, why are these power sources essential for the truck? The diesel engine cannot remain on in individual states for only a few minutes. New York is one of the states with this law. "6 NYCRR Subpart 217-3 (leaves DEC website probits heavy- duty vehicles, including non-diesel and diesel trucks and buses with a gross weight rating (GVWR) of more than 8,500 pounds, from idling for more than five minutes at a time.

DEC Conservation Officer enforces the idling regulation."[6] If a driver is caught running their truck to stay warm or cold, they are ticketed and issued a monetary fine. Humanity is no longer present globally; if the government would prefer a human to freeze or overheat versus using available devices for comfort.

The industry does have special custom-made trucks. These trucks have all the amenities of a home. The semi-trucks include a bathroom, shower, full refrigerator, confectionary ovens, dishwasher, washer and dryer, and extra closet space. These trucks must have a generator to support the additional equipment inside. In-motion satellite systems and rooftop air are other features.

---

[5] 5 Kevin Robertson, A Beginner's Guide to Hotshot Trucking (Nashville, TN: Robertson, 2017), 12.

[6] New York State, Department of Environmental Conservation, dec.ny.gov., 01/20/2020.

As the trucking industry's demand increased, trucks' need to park and drivers to rest became a vital part of the industry. The driver was often away from home for two to three months. Therefore, there is an immediate need for driver services. The drivers need showers, restaurants, supplies, fuel, and other services. Remember, the trucks are not equipped with showers; therefore, showers are placed in the facilities to service the drivers. Many times before and after a long day's work, the driver park at the truck stop to relax and enjoy a hot shower.

> "There's a certain way of thinking and feeling which is in every driver's blood; it's there when you schedule a long haul, and it's there when you finally get a shower after a 4-day run. It's there when you're driving in the morning with the whole world out in front of you, just waiting to be experienced, and it's there when you are on the dark, quiet highway in the middle of nowhere, wondering what your family and friends are doing" (Ryder 2021, 3).[7]

Semi-truck parking continues to challenge the industry. Imagine working all day, and the area is not equipped with a truck stop. These men and women must sleep in vacant parking lot, highway off-ramps, and business parking lots. Although the semi- truck has heat and air, the drivers cannot utilize those functions in some states. When an average person hears these restrictions, governmental agencies fail to understand basic human needs. Parking is an essential part of driver needs in the industry. However, throughout the country, there continues to be a shortage of parking and facilities to service the drivers.

Truck Parking

Over two hundred drivers park at truck stops on any given day. Evangelism opportunities develop in churches willing to reach out and support the community.

Evangelism is more than passing out flyers one time to a

---

[7] Joe Ryder, CDL Minded Marketing (Nashville, TN: Ryder, 2021), 3.

location, evangelism is being a consistent presence in an organization. The truck stop in some areas contains more significant buildings with office space. Some truck stops have additional stores open for drivers. A few have beauty shops and barbershops.

Truck Drivers are only allowed to work 14 hours a day, and out of the 14 hours, the driver can operate the vehicle for 11 hours. During these 11 hours, the driver must take a 30-minute break. The break allows the driver to eat, have restroom facilities, and rest. Therefore, some trucks are in and out of the truck stop all day while others are present overnight or longer. During these breaks, the driver can communicate with others at the truck stop.

Each year, some truck stops have driver appreciation day, and many local trucking companies do. Evangelism at a driver appreciation could contain passing out the gifts some companies have purchased for their drivers. Some companies host barbecues for the drivers. The ministry could donate a commodity to the business or help cook the drivers' food. Once a relationship is developed, a church could open its doors to host an event creating a lasting relationship.

Current Truckstop Ministry

Some truck stop ministries are present on site. Only a few of the truck stop has an active church ministry. Walcott IA truck stop has one of the better truck stop ministries. The group is available to assist the drivers with a professional office. However, the trucking industry needs more churches, Pastors, and ministries to donate time and resources to the truck drivers. As the world evolves, opportunities for evangelism change. Churches must think outside the box. However, many of the ministries are not present to assist drivers. The Church must adapt to the change in society. The leaders must realize the community consists of those who are not residents but have businesses catering to visitors. During a survey, a driver who is a non-believer felt a ministry would be helpful to the community.

Is A Full-Service Ministry Needed in the Truckstops?

Recently, a survey asked if a full-service ministry would benefit the truck stops. The responses contain a positive response to a truck stop ministry. Most survey takers believed that a ministry would enhance the truck stop because of the driver's religious beliefs. The survey thought it's beneficial in helping drivers in difficult situations while away from home. The ability to fellowship with others will help to enhance one's spiritual formation. "For where two or three are gathered together in my name, there am I in the midst of them" (Matt. 24:20 KJV). The Bible encourages Christians to come together and worship together.

21st Century

The Church is in the 21st Century; although humanity's needs are the same, the Church's demands have increased. God created the Church to support the community. From ancient times to now, the Church, known for its hope, displayed over centuries. God provided hope when the Children of Israel were in Egypt in bondage. God provided hope with Meshack; Shadrack and Abednego were in the fiery furnace. God provided hope when African Americans were taken from their native home. God provided hope when Martin Luther King sought equality for African Americans.

Therefore, the goal is the development of "A Truckstop Religious Resource Center." Many drivers need to experience the hope others felt from God throughout the centuries. These drivers need resources available to them to assist with their emotional journey. The resources center is present more than Sunday Morning Service and Bible Study. Counseling services will help support many drivers who suffer from an illness or emergency family issues.

Social Equality and Diversity

The truck stops are a diverse group of individuals. "Diversity refers to differences among social groups such as ethnic heritage, class, age, gender, sexuality, ability, religion, and nationality."[8] The truck driver's community consists of an incredibly diverse community. It is essential to have a clear perspective of the audience. Along with the different cultures come additional requirements. The leader must evaluate the truck stop in their area to learn the men's and women's needs. Therefore, the leader must provide the proper training to ministry participants. Ethical and moral practice allows the participants to understand the community's demographic. It is vital to have a well-rounded program that meets the desires of a culturally diverse society.

Equality is vital. The community expects any organization to understand that all truck drivers expect equal treatment. Some communities suffer when cultures which are singled out because of their race and religious beliefs. Therefore, the Church must accept all cultures. The Church must remain open to everyone and treat everyone with respect. The leader must choose people who understand and believe in equality versus division.

The body of Christ consists of various cultures, and humanity is present to learn from one another. The truck stop ministry provides many learning opportunities and challenges for a church. Evangelizing opens the eyes of leaders and participants and gives a new perspective on the world's needs. However, equal treatment must remain the focus of anyone working in the ministry.

Women Truck Driver

Truck driving, for years, has been a male-dominated industry. Most of the items in the truck stops supported the needs of men. Women have begun to work in the industry for the past ten years. The change in women working in the industry forced the truck stops to review their products and services. The truck stops could no longer cater to males; the essential women's products helped satisfy female drivers' needs.

"Gender diversity brings a new perspective, fuels greater idea generation, problem-solving and innovation, increasing business performance and overall revenue generation. Gain access to relevant market intelligence, content, networking, collaboration, and best

---

[8] Marianna Adams and Lee Anne Bell, Teaching for Diversity and Social Justice (New York, NY: Routledge, 2016), 2.

practices to help achievement. Many companies are reaping the benefits of solid workforce diversity".[9]

The industry demographic has changed throughout the years. Current ministries focus on males to evangelize. Women evangelists relate to the challenges women face daily. However, working with women at a truck stop may pose additional challenges. Women truck drivers face verbal abuse and sexual insults. Because many men are on the road for weeks and months, sexual comments have become frequent. Therefore, verbal and sexual abuse meetings would provide awareness to female drivers. Women's social services allow women to discuss their challenges while on the road. Creating a database and offering zoom classes for female drivers is beneficial.

Summary

Leaders must know their audience. Although each truck stop is different in layout, the truck drivers' requirements remain the same. Just because the community is a transit community, the driver suffers from the same human emotions others face. The first important fact most leaders must realize is that the drivers cannot physically come to the Church because of their vehicles' size. Therefore, the leader must think outside the box and develop a ministry to allow the Church to present itself at the truck stop.

The truck driver's community is diverse and requires individuals who can communicate effectively and understand there are no racial barriers. These leaders must reframe from seeing color but focus on the souls of the individuals who come to the community. Racial barriers must never present themselves to the Church of God. God was love and hope. Therefore, anyone who works in the ministry must follow God's teachings as an example for His people.

Biblical counseling is an essential aspect of the world. God is wise and knows what is beneficial to each human being. Therefore, developing a relationship with God allows a person to have a personal connection. God strives to see His creations turn to Him and seek wisdom in all situations. Secular counseling will not allow the counselee to reach their full potential.

The Bible is essential in counseling. The counselor needs to

---

[9] Women in Trucking. Website, womenintrucking.org. 1/30/2020

use the entire Bible and reframe from providing counseling when not led by God. "The believer and unbeliever need the truth; therefore, the counselor must have the ability to interpret the Scripture and pray for wisdom from God. God's grace and mercy for His creation allow humanity to seek spiritual formation from God." [10]Therefore, a biblical counselor has the individual's soul as their first interest in saving an individual. The purpose of this chapter was to provide an overview of the trucking industry.

---

[10] Julie Smith, *Biblical and Secular Counseling* (Charlotte, NC: Charlotte: Charlotte Christian College and Theologian Seminary, 2021).

Chapter Ten
Conclusion

Based on this dissertation's hypostasis, *If the church supports truck drivers by conveying love and biblical ministries such as counseling, evangelism could enhance discipleship within the church body*. This dissertation has proved that a stable truck stop ministry is needed in the truck stops. The dissertation consists of nine chapters that provide detailed facts discussing the need for a ministry within a truck stop. This chapter will give an overview of the pertinent facts in the previous chapters proving that a Truck Stop Ministry is critical for the truck stops to support the drivers. The focal Scripture for this dissertation is Luke 14:23, "and the Lord said unto the servant, Go out into the highways and hedges, and compel them to come in, that my house will be filled."

Chapter one provided a detailed purpose and need for this dissertation. This chapter laid out the dissertation's process and the information provided. The key to this chapter is that it explained that the dissertation would include letters from addicts describing many struggles. Although many professionals have studied the effects and struggles of addictions, the letters from addicts were essential to gaining a truck driver's perspective of the need for a truck stop ministry.

Chapter two focuses on the professional's understanding of addictions. The literature in the books explains the research on addictions throughout the years. When researching the topic, no information was available that discussed a truck stop ministry.

Therefore, to prove the importance of a truck stop ministry, various sources were put together to display the ministries' needs. The literature provided biblical counseling, evangelism, drug addiction, obesity, and sexual desires addictions. This information provided support to the need for a truck stop ministry.

Chapter three is the focal point of the dissertation, and this chapter provided proof from many respondents of the struggles faced by their addictions. The respondents opened their stories to this project to give an addict insight into their experiences. This information was vital in understanding a person's struggle; each respondent felt having a truck stop ministry was critical. Another positive factor about this chapter is that it provided that individuals living within the area of the truck stop would also be open to participating in counseling at the truck stop. Respondent three was seeking help and an understanding of addictions. A truck stop in the area would have allowed respondent three to discuss and gain insight into their situation.

Chapter four explained the importance of evangelism. As leaders, the purpose of ministry is to help others.

> "According to McVey and Quarles, there are hurting people all around you, even in your own family. It doesn't matter who you are or what you know. God will use you if you do these five essential things. First, accept them just the way they are. Second, have a ministry of grace. Third, tell them who they are in Christ. Fourth, teach them their authority in Christ and how to resist Satan. Lastly, tell them the truth that they are already free and have been given the victory."[1]

The importance of gaining a proper understanding of evangelism is remaining truthful to the ministry and guiding those who may feel lost in understanding the presents of God. This chapter was vital to understanding there is a need for a truck stop ministry. Luke 14:23 tells a person to *go out into the highway*. These men and women are on the highways daily, serving many communities and delivering vital goods. Therefore, a ministry is needed to provide love to those who travel the roads.

This chapter looked at the biblical counseling needs in a truck stop ministry. The Bible is present to offer help and hope to others.

According to Collins, the Bible condemns drunkenness, alcohol abuse, uncontrolled lust, and gluttony. Still, it does not make specific references to drug abuse, eating disorders, or most other addictions that concern us today. We might wonder how those biblical writers would respond if they returned to earth and saw how so many of us are held in the grip of power like the internet, video games, or uncontrolled purpose-driven lifestyles. Before they died, the biblical writers were inspired by the Holy Spirit to give us principles for living, including the following that could apply to any addiction that might be present now

---

[1] Steve McVey and Mike Quarles, *Helping Other Overcome Addictions How's God's Grace Brings Lasting Freedom* (Eugene, OR: Harvest House, 2012), 98-99.

or arise in the future."[2]

Chapter five is essential to understanding the effect drugs have on an addict's brain and body, and a person must know medical terminology and the impact of drugs on the brain. Chapter five states that the brain is connected to and controls the central nervous system, and the system controls the ability of a driver to maintain a commercial vehicle. Therefore, a ministry could assist a driver in understanding and seeking help to overcome their addictions.

> "According to Collins, nobody starts out to be a substance abuser, and most people who develop addictions never expect that this would happen. Initially, the person is induced to try a new experience through the combined influence of family, personal heroes, peer group, cultural environment, curiosity, or psychological needs. Depending on the substance or the individual, people are impacted differently. Often a person will try the drug or new experience once or twice but never get hooked. In other cases, the initial experimentation leads to small steps that follow a downward progression involving behavior change, physical deterioration, family stress, financial problems, career destruction, and increasing psychological disintegration."[3]

This dissertation does not end with the information gathered, and plenty of other struggles can be opened in a truck stop ministry.

Chapters six through eight listed addictions that have affected truck drivers. For a ministry to become successful, a person must understand addiction. These chapters discussed the history and the problems caused by addictions. A person must know the types of addiction and how it hinders an addict's ability to function in society. One fact discovered in this research is that all drugs and actions have positive reactions to humanity; however, abusing medications or activities causes addictions. Chapter nine provides an understanding of the community. Leaders must know their audiences to provide a stable ministry.

---

[2] Gary Collins, *Christian Counseling A Comprehensive Guide* (Nashville, TN: Thomas Nelson, 2007), 682.

[3] Ibid., 690.

Respondent Eight

The goal of Respondent Eight is to provide information about their struggles. Respondent Eight wanted to ensure that his name was included in the letter because he no longer has to hide behind an addiction. He faced his addiction which included his understanding of himself. Troy McKnight's story will prove that biblical counseling is essential in the spiritual growth of any addict. A truck stop ministry would have great success for others.

My drug addiction began when I was in grammar school. I lived in Chicago, Illinois, and I started associating with peers who drank. However, I didn't realize that drinking would result in another addiction that caused me many struggles. I wish I had had a ministry that could have dealt with drug addictions, and maybe my life would have been different. After I began to drink, I then began to use recreational drugs. The continual use led me to develop an addiction that was extremely difficult to overcome. I went through high school suffering from addiction. However, the struggle continued to plague my ability to function when I graduated. My body felt that I needed the drug to function. Once I became an adult, I began to understand that I didn't need to drink and do drugs, but the ability to stop was difficult. I tried to quit alone, but the craving still overtook my desire to stop.

I began to visit ministries on Sunday and prayed that I would be able to stop using drugs. I attended church on Sunday, fellowshipping and praising God. I was back at the drug house Sunday evening, obtaining and smoking cocaine and drinking alcohol. I struggled for years to overcome this addiction. I utilized a word I kept near me to remind me of the power of God. The word I used was "PUSH." PUSH stands for "Pray Until Something Happens." I prayed and prayed, and one Sunday, when I left the church, I realized I didn't have the desire to head to the drug house. I went home, packed up my belongings, and moved from the environment that could cause me to relapse. Going back was not an option for me, and today I hold tight to remaining clean of drugs.

Now I don't feel the craving any longer. I have been clean for 25 years. There was a time when I wouldn't have been able to discuss my addiction. But now I understand the importance. If this story helps one person, my struggle will achieve something. There were consequences for my action, my health did deteriorate, but I remained focused on God. If God can heal me from an addictive drug, I know he can heal my body. I am a local truck driver, and having a spiritual-based ministry within the truck stop can help overcome addictions. Prayer helps me, and anyone willing to listen can overcome their addiction.

Comments on Respondent Eight

Respondent Eight witnesses how one can overcome addictions through biblical counseling. McKnight's story provided a great conclusion to this dissertation. If the church opens its hearts to truck drivers and starts displaying love to those suffering from addiction, souls can be saved. As McKnight grew, he developed the ability to communicate his story. Yearly, McKnight post on his Facebook page the number of years he has been clean of his addiction. His goal is to show others that they can be clean of drugs. This dissertation has proved that a ministry is needed at the truck stops.

Summary

This dissertation has provided the information needed to begin a truck stop ministry. To implement a successful truck stop ministry, the leaders must have committed volunteers who are comfortable with evangelism outside the church. Once the team of volunteers has been selected, training is essential. It is important to have people who can go out to the truck stops and observe the community. Numbers 13:2 God instructed Moses to send men out to explore the land of Canaan. What is extremely essential in this Scripture in Numbers, Moses sent one person from each tribe. This scripture provides an example of the importance of diversity.

By only sending one person to the truck stop, the leader will have one perspective of the community. Therefore, it is important to send a diverse group of individuals to the truck stop. The goal is to obtain as much information as possible to prepare an effective ministry. During these visits, it is important to obtain the name or names of the individuals who are responsible for giving approval to the ministry. Once this process is over, prepare a presentational letter requesting permission to offer spiritual services and counseling to the truck drivers. This is the beginning process of creating the ministry.

Once the church has permission, begin to prepare the ministry. Remember some of the churches will need to team up with other churches to create an effective ministry. Lastly, pray and allow God to guide and lead in preparing an effective ministry. Luke 14:23 remind all leaders and members of their responsibility to the church. The church is to go into the world and seek disciples.

Title Of the Study

Biblical Counseling, An Essential Part of a Truck Stop Ministry

Researcher

Julie Smith

Doctor of Ministry Program

Charlotte Christian College and Theological Seminary (708) 662-0556

jbsmith@charlottechristian.edu

PURPOSE OF STUDY

The study aims to prove a need for a truck stop ministry and biblical counseling within truck stops. This study will include professional references to addictions along with respondents' stories of true-life experiences.

STUDY PROCEDURES

Each respondent is asked to write about their struggle with addictions. Please include your first drug experience (for example, at home, as a child, in adulthood, or while driving a truck). What were some of your experiences while dealing with drugs? Are you dealing with a spouse on drugs? Would a truck stop ministry assist you in dealing with your addiction?

The paper should be no longer than four pages long. The paper should be emailed to julie_bibbs@yahoo.com. At the time of receipt, an email will be forwarded confirming.

VALUE

One may ask, what is the value of participating in this study? Writing is beneficial. Writing allows a person to express their views and deal with some of the struggles a person is facing. Please remember that any study of this fashion aims to help others. Your story could change another person's perspective of their addiction.

Participant initials_____

CONFIDENTIALITY

For this study, all information obtained is confidential. All names will be omitted from the study. Each study will be labeled a respondent along with a number. All information will be kept in a confidential file. Any incidents will be reported immediately that could compromise the data.

Thank you for volunteering for this study. Please remember this study provides facts about addictions and the importance of a truck stop ministry. Your information will be immediately destroyed if you decide you are no longer interested in participating in this study. If you have any questions or wish to verify the study, don't hesitate to contact the Charlotte Christian College and Theological Seminary Program Director, Dr. Wesley McCarter, at (704) 334-6880.

CONSENT

I have read the information provided and understand this study is voluntary. I know I can withdraw anytime, and my data is confidential. I give my consent to include my information in the study. I understand it is voluntary.

Participant's signature _____Date _____

Investigator's signature_____Date _____

Bibliography

Adams, Marianne, and Bell, Lee Anne. *Teaching for Diversity and Social Justice* New York, NY: Routledge. 2016.

Aden, Leroy. *Pastoral Care and the Gospel in the Church and Pastoral Care* Grand Rapids, MI: Baker. 1988.

Anthony, Michael. *Introduction Christian Education: Foundations for the Barr Margaret The Jossey.* Hoboken, NJ: Wiley. 1990.

Belleville, Linda. *Women Leaders and the Church Three Crucial Question* Grand Rapids, MI: Baker. 2000.

Benz, Jonathan, and Robb-Dover, Kristina. *The Recovery-Minded Church Loving and Ministering to People with Addictions.* Downers Grove, IL: IVP Books. 2018.

Black, David. *Using New Testament Greek in Ministry; A Practical Guide for Students And Pastors* Grand Rapids, MI: Bakers Book House. 1993.

How to Write Learning Objectives Using Bloom's Taxonomy, https://ep.jhu.edu/blooms.

Brady, Carol. *Understanding Learning Styles: Providing the Optimal Learning Experience.* International Journal of Childbirth Education. 2013.

Browning, Robert, and Reed, Roy. *Forgiveness, Reconciliation, and Moral Courage: Motives and Designs for Ministry in a Trouble World.* Cambridge City, MA: Eerdmans. 2004.

Bersoff, J.M. *Ethical Conflict in Psychology.* Washington D. C.: American Psychology Association. 2003.

Capps Donald's. *Giving Counsel: A Minister's Guidebook.* St. Louis, MO: Chalice Press. 2001.

Carter, James, and Trull, Joe. *Ministerial Ethics: Moral Formation for Church Leaders.* Grand Rapids, MI: Baker Academic, 2004.

Calhoun, Adele. *Spiritual Disciplines Handbook*. Downer Grove, IL: IVP Books, 2005.

Chand, Samuel. *Bigger Faster Leadership; Lessons from the Builders of the Panama Canal* Nashville, TN: Thomas Nelson. 2017.

Clinton, Dr. Tim, and Hawkins, Dr. Ron. *The Popular Encyclopedia of Christian Counseling: An Indispensable Tool for Helping People with Their Problems*. Eugene, OR: Harvest Home. 2011.

Conn, Harvie, and Ortiz, Manuel. *Urban Ministry: The Kingdom. The City & the People of God*. Downers Grove, IL: IVP Academic. 2001.

Corey, Gerald, and Corey, Marianne, and Callanan, Patrick. *Issues and Ethics in Helping Professions*. Belmont, TN: Brooks/Cole Cengage Learning. 2007.

Corey, Gerald. *Theory and Practice of Counseling and Psychotherapy*, India: Cengage. 2013.

Diesel.net. *Early History of the Diesel Engine*. diselnet.com/tech/diesel history, 2019.

Defenbarge, Jami. *Truck Stop Ministry Bring Faith to The Road Weary*. *Journal*, stitoday.com. 2008.

Dewey, John. *Experience and Education*. New York, NY: FP Free Press. 1938.

DeLange, Elizabeth C. M, and Hammerlund-Udenaes, Margaret, Throne, Robert G. *Drug Delivery to the Brain, Physiological Concepts, Methodologies, and Approaches*. (San Francisco, CA: Springer. 2014.

Earleywine, Mitch *Understanding Marijuana. A New Look at Scientific Evidence*. New York, NY: Oxford University. 2002.

Enns, Paul. *The Moody Handbook of Theology*. Chicago, IL: Moody Publishers. 2014.

Fields, Lee. *Hebrew For the Rest of Us*. Grand Rapids: Zondervan. 2008.

Fee, Gordon. *Discovering Biblical Equality: Complementarity Without Hierarchy*. Downers Grove: InterVarsity Press. 2005.

Geisler, Norman. *Christian Ethics: Contemporary Issues & Options*. Grand Rapids: Bakers Academic. 2010.

Graves, Emily, and Graves, Ritchie. *Teacher Characteristics of Culturally Responsive Pedagogy*. National Association of Culturally Responsive Pedagogy. Article. 2012.

Gruden, Wayne. Christian Ethics: *An Introduction to Biblical Reasoning*. Wheaton: Crossway. 2018.

Guthrie, Shirley. *Christian Doctrine*. Louisville: Westminster John Knox Press. 1973. Harrison, Clement. Trucking Business. Nashville: Harrison. 2020.

Hull, Bill. *The Disciple-Making Pastor; Leading Others on the Journey of Faith*. Grand Rapids: Baker Books. 2007.

Jensen, Irving. *Jensen's Survey of the New Testament*. Chicago: Moody Press. 1977.

_____ *Jensen's Survey of the Old Testament*, Chicago: Moody Press. 1975.

Kaplan, Helen, *The Sexual Desire Disorders: Dysfunctional Regulation of Sexual Motivation* (New York, NY: Routledge, 2015).

Keller, Timothy. *Center Church; Doing Balanced Gospel-Centered Ministry in Your City*. Grand Rapids, MI: Zondervan. 2012.

Mack, Wayne. *A Practical Guide for Effective Biblical Counseling*. Wapwallopen, Pa: Sheppard, 2021.

McVey, Steve, and Quarles, Mike. *Helping Others Overcome Addictions: How God's Grace Brings Lasting Freedom.* Eugene, OR: Harvest House. 2011.

OOIDA.com, hhtp://ooida.com.

Robertson, Kevin. *A Beginner's Guide to Hotshot Trucking.* Nashville, TN: Robertson. 2017.

Ryder, Joe. *CDL Minded Marketing.* Nashville, TN: Ryder. 2021.

Ryder, Colton. *How to Start a Trucking Company,* Nashville, TN: Ryder. 2019.

Schunk, Dale. Social Cognitive Theory; An Agentic Perspective. Columbia: Pearson. 2009.

Smith, Jason, and Smith, Hunt. *Understanding Addiction, Know Science, No Stigma* Visual, 2021.

Smith, Julie. *Paul's Ministry Review,* Charlotte: Charlotte Christian College and Theologian Seminary. PS701 Biblical Theology of Ministry.

Thompson, James W. *Pastoral Ministry According to Paul: A Biblical Vision.* Grand Rapids, MI: Baker Academic. 2006.

Thurman, Howard. *With Head and Heart.* New York, NY: Harcourt Brace & Company. 1979.

Tyndale. New Bible Dictionary. Wheaton: Inter-Varsity Press. 1982.

Women In Trucking. Website. womenintrucking.org.

Zane, Pratt, and Sills, David. Walters and Jeff. *Introduction to Global Missions.* Nashville, TN: B & H Group. 2014.

www.ingramcontent.com/pod-product-compliance
Lightning Source LLC
Chambersburg PA
CBHW071005120626
46546CB00003B/943